MW01717290

A CHAIN OF EVENTS

The Origin & Evolution of Disc Golf

By

Jim Palmeri

Author

&

Phil Kennedy

Editing, Design & Graphics

Wormhole
PUBLISHERS

Wethersfield, Connecticut

A CHAIN OF EVENTS

The Origin & Evolution of Disc Golf

By Jim Palmeri and Phil Kennedy

Published by: **Wormhole Publishers**
181 Ridge Road, Wethersfield, CT 06109-1045

Orders: Use order form at back of book or visit www.FlatFlip.com

Editor: Phil Kennedy   Assistant Editor: Pat Kennedy

Photography: Phil Kennedy

Design & Production: Phil Kennedy, Graphic Images, www.FlatFlip.com

First Printing: July 2015

Printed in U.S.A.

Publishers Cataloging In Publication Data.

Palmeri, Jim, 1942–

A Chain of Events: the origin & evolution of disc golf / by Jim Palmeri—1st ed.

SUMMARY: Two of the early discoverers and players of flying disc games, both leading authorities on the history and collecting of plastic flying discs, collaborate to relate the discovery, early history, and growth of the popular sport of Disc Golf; illuminated with a colorful collection of early flying discs.

Includes index and bibliography.

1. Flying discs (Game)   I. Kennedy, Phil, 1947–, joint author.   II. Title

Dewey Decimal System Number: 796.2

ISBN: 978-0-9774517-0-8 (pbk.)

TABLE OF CONTENTS

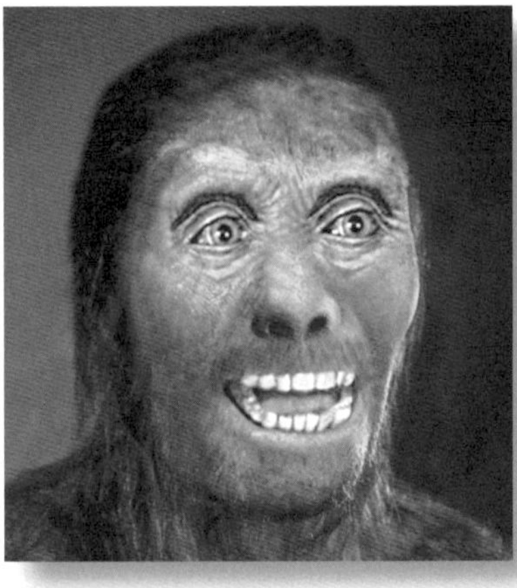

This book is dedicated to

Ooog

the very first hominin
to pick up and hurl
a disc-shaped object

...just for fun!

Preface

W*HEN THE PLUTO PLATTER FIRST FLEW* into the world it was truly as if it were from outer space...an alien toy, unlike anything else we knew. The instructions that were engraved on the underside of the disc gave only the most minimal hint of its potential:

PLAY CATCH—INVENT GAMES.
TO FLY, FLIP AWAY BACKHANDED,
FLAT FLIP FLIES STRAIGHT,
TILTED FLIP CURVES—EXPERIMENT!

No words wasted here. (Maybe they had to pay by the letter for the mold engraving?) But that was all that was needed. And, we immediately loved the way it spun out of our hand and sailed away, apparently free of gravity! It was a gift from the gods! And it was a gift that kept on giving. No sooner were we sailing the colorful discs back and forth than we almost immediately began to follow the invitation to invent games.

Nobody invented new games for tennis balls, hockey pucks, or footballs. Those games were set in stone. But this playful platter almost begged to be used in wonderful new ways. Almost every new group of players came up with its own favorite way to play. On rainy days, when nobody came to the pool, lifeguards filled their time with Olympic-style games of jumping off of the high dive and trying to catch as many discs as they could on the way down.

Details of the "rules" changed with every session of play. Kids at camp put together a team game that was such fun that they dubbed it the "ultimate" game. There was nothing like it!

And, as you will soon see in this book, there were also players who quickly thought that this amazing flying saucer could improve on games that we already knew and loved. It is one of those connections that has turned out to be among the very best. Take the Royal and Ancient game of golf and add to it... the magical flying disc. *Shazam!* An incredible combination. Like most genius ideas, this one almost defines itself. Say, "Hey, let's play golf with a Frisbee!" and the rules seem to write themselves. How that all got started is the amazing story that Jim and Phil will share with us in these pages. You will see how that very potent combination of our old friend, ball golf (let's just call it "bolf" for now) and the flying disc, turned out to be a match truly made in the heavens.

Hey, bolf is a great game, and it's been around in one form or another since the Middle Ages. They've had quite a while to sort it out. But, in the short time that we've been experimenting with discs, we've discovered some positively wonderful advantages to playing golf our own way. For one, it's a whole lot easier to see the disc in flight. That turns out to be a pretty big deal. Sure, bolf is big on TV, but disc golf is really more telegenic. Commentators struggle (while whispering) to explain what those pro bolfers are thinking. The strategies of a disc golfer are much more diverse and visually obvious. To solve the same approach shot challenge, one player of a disc golf group throws a huge hyzer bomb while the next throws a slow roller through the trees and the third, a hard, skipping flight that curves right up into the basket. That...is great television!

Our players will be media stars because it's just much easier to understand and appreciate what they are doing (and thinking).

And, just as it was in the very beginning, the flight of the disc continues to fascinate. While the ball is a slave to the pull of the earth, the disc defies both gravity and our expectations. At their best, the fairways of disc golf courses are not point-to-point grass alleys, but rather are a multiplicity of soaring air routes that require skillful control, power, and finesse to navigate successfully. It's simply a more complex and challenging game, both mentally and physically.

So, with that audacious claim in mind, let's enjoy a delightful trip back to the origins of Disc Golf. It's still the wonderful and ancient game…now evolved to a whole new level of wonder and played as the gods intended.

—Dan "Stork" Roddick

Introduction

D*ISC GOLF!* If you are familiar with the game, you already know what a great competitive sport and recreational activity it is. If you are not familiar with Disc Golf, you are about to find out what you've been missing!

At one point in time there was no Disc Golf. Anywhere. But today there is a huge culture of Disc Golf spread all around the world, complete with a professional organization and tournament play. So just how did all this come to be? Where did Disc Golf come from? How did the sport get started? If those questions are of interest to you, then you are reading the right book.

Attempts to answer those questions by people who don't really know the facts have led to an appallingly large number of apocryphal stories, half-truths, and just plain wrong information being disseminated in newspaper stories, magazine articles, newscasts, books, and perhaps worst of all, on the Internet. At best, the information is merely out of date and missing newly found material. At worst, the information is totally wrong, pure fiction fabricated out of ignorance, or by people trying to re-write history for personal gain.

This book attempts to cut through all this misinformation and accurately chronicle the specific events that led to the origin and evolution of the sport of Disc Golf.

Of course, the origin of Disc Golf is inextricably linked to the origin of all disc play and *the* Frisbee® itself. So we start with just that—a good overview of the origin of all things to do with flying discs. This topic is fraught with just as much misinformation as is the topic of Disc Golf. We are going to be accurate. We encourage you to compare what you learn here with a lot of the gobbledy-gook you may have heard or read in the past, and then decide for yourself which seems more accurate and makes more sense. We guarantee that you will find no other source of disc information that is more up to date and more accurate than what you will read in this book.

—Jim Palmeri & Phil Kennedy

CHAPTER 1

A CHAIN OF EVENTS

Survival of the Flittest

FROM THE VERY DAWN of human existence, small disc-shaped objects have accompanied mankind's technological progress and cultural development. These objects either existed in nature, or were man-made artifacts, and they varied widely in their aerodynamic flight characteristics. Some were clunkers, while others were quite Frisbee-like in their capacity to skim through the air.

No one can ever know when or where the very first human picked up a flyable disc-shaped object and flung it. It must have occurred during the prehistoric age of mankind, so by definition there is no written record of such a happening...but it obviously *did* happen.

From what we *do* know from the archaeological record and first-hand observations of human behavior, we can infer that when any group from any period of human history happened upon hand-holdable disc-shaped objects, eventually someone picked one up and flung it. It could have been something as simple as a streambed stone worn smooth by rushing water, or a dried buffalo chip thrown in jest. Later came clay dishes, carved wooden bowls, woven mats, leather caps, felt hats, pot tops, can lids, cake pans, pie tins, cardboard ice cream container tops, etc., etc. It was inevitable.

Discobolis statue and ancient Greek discus

History does provide solid evidence of disc flinging going as far back as 708 B.C.[1] Records exist that confirm the discus throw was part of the ancient Greek pentathlon event. This proves that people from even earlier ages showed an interest in scaling disc-shaped objects. If disc flinging activities were popular enough among the ancient Greeks to become incorporated into their early Olympic competition over 2,720 years ago, similar activities more than likely occurred in other ancient cultures as well, if not in an organized manner, at least informally. It is virtually certain that this sort of disc flinging activity continued to occur throughout the ages of human existence.

Some of the disc-shaped objects that were flung in antiquity would have sailed through the air with fascinating aerodynamic flight patterns. Eventually, some bystanders would have noticed the intriguing way the discs flew through

1. http://en.wikipedia.org/wiki/Discus_throw

the air and exclaimed something to the effect of "Wow that was neat! Let me try that."

Within that set of people who wanted to try flinging a disc-shaped object themselves, some would have been successful at duplicating the "neat" flight. The fun of this activity would have enticed some of them to continue the flinging activity on a regular basis simply for the fun of it. That's basic human nature. When you discover something that is fun to do, you do it again, and repeat the activity until it no longer turns you on.

Within the set of people regularly flinging a flying disc, some of them would have discovered the efficiency of tossing it back and forth with another person in a catch-and-throw type of activity.

Within this set of people playing catch with a flying disc, some would have been creative and invented games to make their tossing and catching all the more fun and interesting.

A purely conjectural exercise will demonstrate what I mean by all that. Imagine it is 1865, and a group of kids are playing on a village green somewhere. The mother of one of the kids brings a tin of cookies as a treat for the children to enjoy. They eat all the cookies, and as the mother is about to leave, she calls out to her son, "Johnny, please bring me the cookie can lid." He complies, but instead of carrying it over to her, he flings it toward her in an effort to save time because he wants to get back to playing with his friends.

The lid just happens to sail toward his mother in a classically beautiful Frisbee-like flight. Another lad observes this and exclaims, "Wow! Did you see that! Let me try!" He scurries over to the tin lid before the mother can retrieve it and flings it back towards Johnny, who catches it in mid-air and flings it back once more. Now all the kids are exclaiming, "Let me try it!" "Throw it to me!" "My turn!" The kids have great fun with their newly discovered activity, but want more action than what one lid can provide. Johnny asks his mother if she has more such lids in the kitchen. She replies, "Maybe," but warns the children to be careful not to get hit in the head with that cookie can lid!

Over a period of time, the kids gather a variety of disc-shaped tin and cardboard lids to keep on hand for their flinging fun. They begin to develop good throwing and catching skills. They create more disc-tossing activities and begin challenging each other to games like "I bet I can sail it farther than you." Or, "I bet I can catch it more times in a row without dropping it than you can." Or, "I bet you I can fling it to that tree in fewer throws than it takes you to do it."

The parents of these kids, worried about what neighbors might think, suppress their urge to try this "childish" activity in front of other adults, and then when they are alone with their kids and no one is looking, they secretly indulge in some lid-flinging fun.

This fictitious conjecture represents only one of the unlimited possible realities of mankind's interrelationship with hand-held disc-shaped objects that must have occurred throughout the ages. Some accounts of early interaction with disc-shaped objects have been well documented. Victor Malafronte, in his book, *The Complete Book of Frisbee,*[2] goes into detail about many instances of early pre-plastic disc play, some of which are Disc Golf-like in nature.

---

2. Victor Malafronte, *The Complete Book of Frisbee* (Alameda, CA: American Trends Publishing, 1998), pages 22–45

Victor is one of the most important researchers and fact-getters that our sport has ever had, and he did a fabulous job gathering information for his book. If you want more details about early disc play, I highly recommend reading his book.

Victor's findings *do* make one wonder how many other incidences of early disc play occurred that we just don't know about—occurrences that even Victor didn't find out about. The details in Victor's book also make it quite clear that the known incidences of early pre-plastic disc play were *not* responsible for the birth and evolution of today's Frisbee culture. So we still have to ask the question of just where did it all come from? How did it all get started?

Attempts to answer these questions have led to widespread myths of the origins of Frisbee play.

One such myth is that of the Yale undergraduate, Elihu Frisbee. Elihu supposedly rebelled against compulsory chapel attendance by flinging the collection plate across the campus quad. Its amazing flight caused quite a stir, and others wanted to emulate it. Supposedly the word about this activity spread out from the Yale campus and finally developed into today's Frisbee sports and culture.[3] This story is generally taken for what it is—a tongue-in-cheek spoof about the origin of the Frisbee that virtually no one believes is true...except maybe Yale alumni who would love their Alma Mater to get all the credit for starting the Frisbee phenomenon. Sorry, Yalies, it just ain't so.

3. Goldy Norton, *The Official Frisbee Handbook* (New York, NY: Bantam Books, 1972), page 1.

A more seriously taken and very popular story (b wrong) is about Yale students flinging pie pans from the Pie Company in nearby Bridgeport, Connecticut. The Yalies are really looking for some sort of credit! The story goes that this activity caught on as a fad and disc flying spread out from there. But unlike the Elihu Frisbee tale, many people believe this myth is the true account of the beginning of Frisbee play and the Frisbee culture. Almost anywhere you read about Frisbee or a Frisbee-related event, or see something about Frisbee on TV, or on the Internet, the story usually includes the Frisbie Pie Company legend in an effort to give a little background about the origin of the Frisbee. The purveyors of this information usually learned about this myth from the people associated with the Frisbee event they were writing about. Or, they may have Googled "Frisbee history" on the Internet. But either way, the resulting conclusion is always the same: that all Frisbee activities started with the Frisbie bakery in Bridgeport, Connecticut. As much as people would like to believe this myth, this is not the one true way that Frisbee play got started.

A typical tin from the Frisbie Pie Company

In reality the Frisbie bakery was only one of hundreds (thousands?) of pie companies all over the world that have existed in the past two centuries. Pie tins from all those other bakeries were also tossed around in the same manner that the Yalies tossed Frisbie pie tins. And it wasn't only pie tins that were being tossed around, and it wasn't only Yale students tossing them. People everywhere were flinging cookie can lids, candy container lids, potato chip can lids, popcorn can lids, cherry can lids, cardboard ice cream container lids, and innumerable other disc-shaped objects. Remember, this type of disc flinging activity is known to have taken place anywhere and anytime throughout history.

There is however, a small element of truth to this Yale and Frisbie Pie Company myth. There *is* a connection between Yale University, the Frisbie Pie Company, and the actual name "Frisbee," which is universally associated with flying disc activities of any kind. Perhaps the Yalies might get a little credit after all! The truth is that during the 1940s and 1950s, playing toss and catch with tin and cardboard lids did develop into a somewhat faddish recreational activity on many college campuses across the nation—not just the Ivy League campuses and Yale University in particular. It just so happened that on the Yale campus, the easily available Frisbie pie pans were common among the variety of popular flying disc items used by the students. We don't know who was the very first person who ever used the term "Frisbie" to refer to pie pan flinging activity, but given that the word "FRISBIE'S" was stamped into each pie pan in large block letters, it was inevitable that someone would eventually associate the word Frisbie with the activity they were undertaking.

It has been suggested that the students would call out *"FRISBIE!"* as a warning when a metal pie pan was flying toward a person who wasn't aware of the oncoming missile. Regardless of however and wherever the term "frisbie" first got associated with disc-flinging activities, "frisbie" eventually became the generic term for those activities at Yale, Dartmouth, and other Ivy League schools. This is evidenced by a number of newspaper articles in which the phonetically similar terms "friszby," "frisbie," "frisbee," "phrisbee," and "frisby" were all used interchangeably at one time or another in write-ups describing the disc-flinging phenomena during that period of time.

This "frisbie" terminology became so strongly entrenched in the vernacular of the Eastern college campuses that in the 1950s, when the new-fangled plastic Space Saucer and Pluto Platter discs started to show up in the campus bookstores, the Ivy League students ignored their given trade names and also referred to them as "frisbies." Flinging them around and playing catch with them became known as "frisbie-ing." Note these advertisements from the Yale student newspaper:

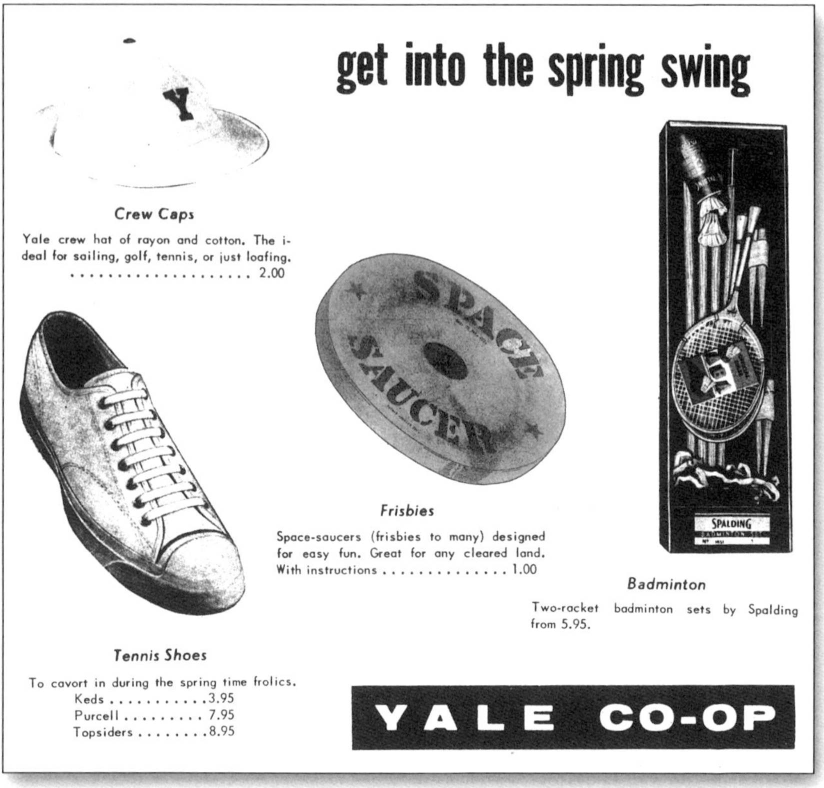

When the Wham-O Manufacturing Company first started selling their Pluto Platter Flying Saucer in 1957, Rich Knerr and Spud Melin, co-owners of the company, kept close tabs on any and all media mention of their new product and others like it.

The May 13, 1957 issue of *Sports Illustrated* published an article with this excerpt:

> A Frisbee is a plastic device shaped like a garbage-can lid, but much smaller (about the size of a dinner plate) and without a handle. Thrown by an expert—and after 10 minutes' practice, anyone is an expert—it can be made to skim lightly

> through the air and pause for an instant, still spinning, over the catcher's head. He plucks it from the air and throws it back, and the resulting game, like the object itself, is called Frisbee.[4] Frisbees can also be made to hook, slice, boomerang, and skip along a sidewalk like a stone on water.

They also noted that:

> The Keebler Biscuit Co. of Philadelphia has been making a prototype of the Frisbee for years, possibly without knowing that it was doing so. Long ago picnickers and beachgoers learned that the lid from a large tin can of Keebler crackers could be made to skim and hover exactly as Frisbees do, and so a game called Keebler Can was invented.

They concluded with:

> Frisbee, too, is known at several schools, though it was Princeton that gave the pastime a local habitation and a name. Nobody at Princeton seems to know who named Frisbee, or why. Nobody, for that matter, seems able to agree on why the students play it. "The cost of materials is low, compared to a ball and glove," was one undergraduate explanation. (Frisbees sell for 79¢ at Princeton.) "It caught on," said another, "because it is childish. It relieves the mind of the tensions of college." "It is a gentleman's game," said a third. "If you are good at it, you can sit in a chair and play."

In the next few weeks *Sports Illustrated* published several letters from readers responding to the article. Excerpts from those:

4. Note the spelling: "Frisbee" not "Frisbie."

> Sirs,
> We at Miami University, Oxford, Ohio, are familiar with the game of Frisbee. We also have variations of Frisbee. These include Night Frisbee, Wandering Frisbee and team, individual or competitive accuracy bouts.

> Sirs:
> Phrisbee has been played on the Amherst campus ever since that fall day in 1949 when a sophomore slipped on the steps of Johnson Chapel and lost control of his tray of a local brew. Several classmates walking nearby were stunned to see that the tray dipped and glided through the air. Determined to investigate this phenomenon, they enlisted the aid of the late physics professor Aaron Phrisbee, who personally supervised experiments on the quad.

On May 16th, 1957, the Redlands, California daily newspaper included a similar article about "Frisbie" play. The article included this excerpt:

> No one has been able to give a satisfactory explanation why these miniature flying saucers are called Frisbies. After intensive research and interviewing, a consensus of findings by known or suspected Frisbians seems to maintain: "It doesn't matter why they are called Frisbies. They just are."

The July 8, 1957 issue of *Time* magazine carried an article captioned "The Name's Frisbee" and contained these excepts:

> Frisbee...was well on its way this week to becoming America's newest sports craze. Played with a brilliantly colored plastic disk, usually 9 inches in diameter and much like a hubcap, its origin is as hazy as its ground rules. The object of the game is simply for one player

> to toss the Frisbee, or disk, into the air and try to keep it from his opponent's grasp. To date, hundreds of thousands of them have been tossed around by gamboling grownups.
>
> Dartmouth and Yale have been at it for two years and Princeton men were Frisbeeing frantically last semester, even pledging their dates with the flying disks.
>
> Over the last alumni weekends, thousands of Princeton old boys flexed their wrists and learned to Frisbee; undergraduates still on campus made a killing by selling these disks at $1 apiece, while during the spring a local stationery store sold 5,300 of them at 79 cents each.
>
> **Cookie Tins, Too:** Just who shot the first Frisbee into the air will probably remain a mystery forever. Spinning cookie-tin tops is an ancient pastime and a generation ago college students frolicked by tossing around pie plates from a baking company named Mrs. Frisbee's Pies. The Frisbee name seems to have stuck longest, although the game is also called Flying Saucers, Space Saucers, Pluto Platters, and Scalo.
>
> Probably the most exquisite variation of all is the one known to Princeton men as "Guts Frisbee," in which, not a plastic saucer, but a rusty 6-inch circular saw blade, is used.

These articles confirm that the terms frisby, frisbie, frizby, frisbee, or whatever variation that was seen in the print media of the 1950s had become the term of choice for people taking part in early disc-flinging activities.

Rich Knerr and Spud Melin thought that the word was a catchy term (no pun intended, but very applicable anyway), and Wham-O decided that they would name their Pluto Platter disc "Frisbee." The name began appearing on the company's printed

Left: 1957 Wham-O Pluto Platter
Right: 1958 Pluto Platter with "Frisbee" name
Below: Late 1957 Wham-O product line card

materials by July 1957, and the next batch of Pluto Platters produced for the 1958 season all had the name Frisbee engraved in large letters on the top side of each disc. Wham-O went on to apply for and receive a trademark for the term "Frisbee," which has been the registered name for all Wham-O flying disc products ever since.

So there is good circumstantial evidence that the *name* associated with today's Frisbee culture indeed came from the Frisbie Pie Company in Bridgeport, Connecticut. But the *name* is the only credit that the Frisbie Pie Company can get towards their contribution to the Frisbee culture. The actual activity of disc flinging goes way back long before William P. Frisbie was even born...much less started his pie company.

Two first style Wham-O Pluto Platters in their packages. The bag on the left was printed in the spring of 1957 before "Frisbee" was used. Later that same year the name was added as shown on the right.

The Frisbee Prevails

SO JUST HOW did the Frisbee phenomenon come about? That is a very interesting question, and we believe that we have an accurate answer for you.

We start by analyzing what had to happen in order for flying discs to be created and for disc flinging to evolve into the world-wide, organized Frisbee culture that exists today. It turns out that there were several key factors that all had to come together before this could happen:

1. There had to be people so enthusiastic about flying disc play that they wanted to share their activity with all their friends and acquaintances.

2. There had to be one or more individuals with entrepreneurial tendencies who recognized that flying disc activities could be marketable.

3. There had to exist an industrial and technological capability to create a ready supply of mass-produced, inexpensive, and durable flying disc items designed for recreational play.

4. There had to be news and communications media in place to help spread the word about flying disc activities.

We have already indicated that at any given time in human history, item number one was fulfilled. From the ancient Greek pentathlon games all the way to twentieth-century pie pan and tin lid tossing, there has been enthusiastic play with all manner of flying disc-type items. But it wasn't until the mid-twentieth century that the other three conditions all came into play at the same time. Only with the coincidence of these three conditions, combined with the first condition, could the Frisbee culture begin to develop and evolve.

The historical record also gives evidence of the existence of item number two. Walter Darby of Great Neck, New York discovered the pleasures of disc flinging in the 1930s. He thought the activity was unique and worthy of a patent, and that it could be marketed for profit. Darby applied for and won a patent for his "Disc Scaling Game," a disc golf type of game complete with basket "holes" in which to "hole out."[1] The problem was the lack of item number three. No matter how much entrepreneurial desire and skill someone may have had, if there was no industrial capacity to create and mass produce suitable flying discs at a reasonable cost, it wasn't going to happen. And history shows that it didn't happen for Walter Darby, or for that matter, anyone else, during that time period.

Items three and four are of more recent development, and again, until they appeared on the scene in conjunction with items one and two, the flying disc couldn't truly fly into mass consciousness.

---

1. Victor Malafronte, *The Complete Book of Frisbee* (Alameda, CA: American Trends Publishing, 1998), page 42.

Walter "Fred" Morrison and Ernest C. "Bill" Robes were two very active and enthusiastic tin lid flingers. Their embodiment of item two is what separated these men from the numerous others in the tin lid era. They both had entrepreneurial ambitions and both thought that flying disc activities could be marketable.

The flying tin lid activities of these two men were strikingly parallel, but they never even knew that each other existed. Both men enjoyed tinkering and inventing things outside of their regular occupations. Fred Morrison was a journeyman construction worker in California; Bill Robes was a teacher and ski coach in New Hampshire. During the 1940s they both enthusiastically enjoyed flinging tin lids as a recreational activity. Fred Morrison got his inspiration from a popcorn can lid, and Bill Robes launched his business ventures with a cherry can lid.

Being the inventors that they were, their entrepreneurial spirit led them to think that plastic versions of their tin lids might be the answer. It just so happened that by the late 1940s the technology of the plastics industry had advanced to the point of being economically feasible for mass producing small plastic items. Both Fred and Bill were cognizant of this development, and looked into ways of creating a plastic version of their tin lids. Their thoughts and goals were the same, but their inventive approaches to creating their very first plastic prototypes were quite different.

Fred Morrison actually started out in 1937.[2] His original introduction to the joys of flinging a flying-disc type of object

2. Fred Morrison and Phil Kennedy, *Flat Flip Files Straight* (Wethersfield, CT: Wormhole Publishers, 2006), page 34. Note: this book is highly recommended for Frisbee history buffs. It is an excellent chronicle of this key part of the origin of disc sports.

is basically a real-life example of our hypothetical story about the kids on the village green discovering the fun of flying around a cookie tin lid. The only differences were that Fred was a young man instead of a young kid, and he was at a Thanksgiving gathering of his girlfriend's family instead of a village green. Someone brought popcorn to the gathering in a popcorn can instead of cookies in a cookie tin. Other than that, it was the very same thing. Someone after dinner tossed the tin popcorn can lid in a Frisbee-like spinning manner. Fred Morrison took notice of its flight. He thought it was neat and did some flinging with it himself. Fred became totally captivated by the activity and kept that particular popcorn can lid in order to repeat the fun another day. Throwing and catching the popcorn can lid became an enjoyable and regular recreational activity for Fred and his girlfriend (and future wife) Lu, an activity that they shared with friends and acquaintances.

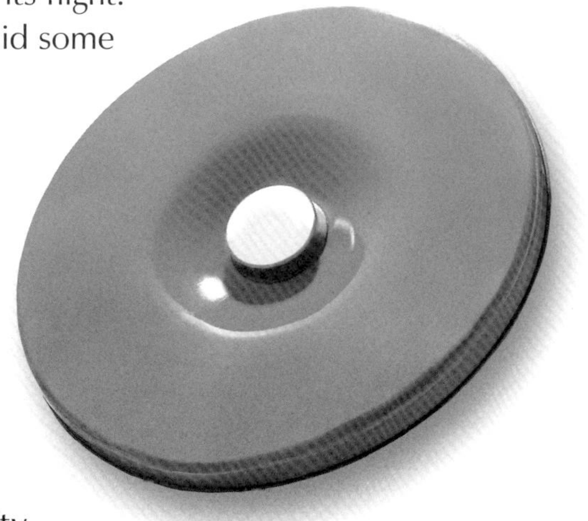

A Geiser's Popcorn can lid

When that popcorn can lid got too battered and bent to be usable anymore, Fred started using cake pans. While Fred and Lu were having fun flying a cake pan at the beach one day, an observer was so taken with their activity that he offered to buy their cake pan for 25 cents, which was a 400% profit over the original five cent cost of the pan.[3] That led Fred to thinking about how he might turn their disc flying activities into a profitable business. His first idea was to make streamlined metal flying discs; then plastic came to mind. But at that period of time, hard, brittle Bakelite was about the only plastic in use; there wasn't a suitable soft, flexible plastic that fit his needs. World War Two came along and Fred put his thoughts on hold while he answered his call of duty. After the war ended, thoughts about creating a plastic flying disc came to the forefront once again, and by then, the plastics industry had developed a more flexible and durable plastic that he could use for his project.

A typical cake pan

Fred Morrison met and partnered with a fellow named Warren Franscioni, who had taken an avid interest in Fred's cake pan flinging activities. Warren agreed with Fred that there might be a lucrative marketing opportunity and offered to work with him and to financially back the project.

They started by machining prototypes of several of Fred's disc designs out of solid blocks of "Tenite" plastic, which became the very first known plastic flying discs. They decided that whichever prototype flew best would be the one they would mass produce.

3. Morrison and Kennedy, *Flat Flip Flies Straight,* page 34.

In 1947, prototype in hand, Fred Morrison and Warren Franscioni contracted with Southern California Plastic, a local plastic injection molding company, to start producing a disc called the "Flyin-Saucer." While the mold was being developed, they decided to call their little business "PIPCO."[4] By early 1948 the first run of Flyin-Saucers became available. As far as we know, these were the very first plastic flying discs ever manufactured and marketed to the public for the sole purpose of playing catch and having fun. Fred and Warren began to experiment with different ways to market their invention.

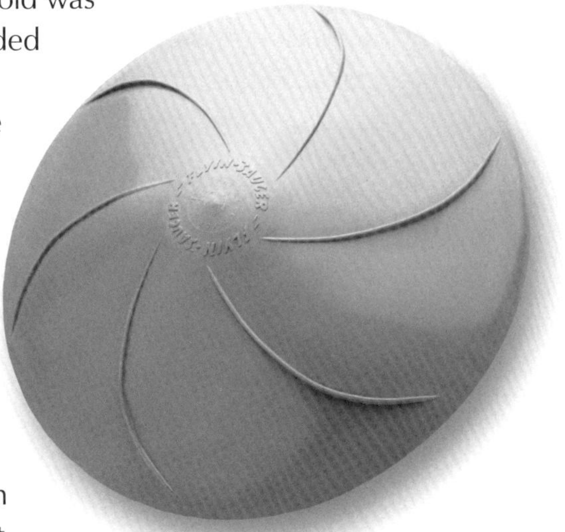

The Flyin-Saucer was designed by Fred Morrison and first issued in the spring of 1948

But not far behind was Bill Robes. Bill was the East Coast counterpart of Fred Morrison. We don't know exactly when Bill Robes first scaled a cherry can lid and realized that it was a fun thing to do, but it was no later than the mid-forties. Bill was an inventor, wood worker, and furniture maker, as well as a world-class skier. His skiing ability led him to the position of ski director at the Kimble Union Academy prep school in 1943. He later became the ski-jumping coach at nearby Dartmouth College.

4. It did *not* stand for "Partners In Plastic" as is widely stated. Fred's inspiration was "If it's a PIPCO product, it's a pip!" A pip in 1947 jargon meant "an excellent thing." See Morrison & Kennedy, *Flat Flip Flies Straight*, page 64.

We don't know for sure whether Robes discovered cherry can lid flinging while observing the students at Kimble Union Academy, or whether it was he that introduced the idea of tin lid scaling to the students at KUA. Whichever way it was, disc flying was a normal part of Kimble Union Academy's recreational activities during the forties, and Bill Robes was in the thick of it.[5]

Many of the KUA students continued their education at Dartmouth where some of them continued their cherry can lid activities. For all we know, it may have been KUA students that introduced the fun of tin lid scaling on the Dartmouth campus during the late forties and early fifties.

Bill Robes strongly felt that scaling a disc-shaped object was a natural urge that all human beings shared. In a 1980 personal interview with Bill Robes, he pointed out that whenever people walk along the shore of a pond or lake and come across a flat disc-shaped stone, they often pick it up and try to skip it across the water. He also claimed that people going to the dump with something like a bunch of old vinyl phonograph records will often fling each record individually because of the fun of watching them fly through the air, rather than just dumping the whole batch at once.

No doubt Bill Robes was talking about his own strong urge to scale disc-shaped objects. His theory that all human beings shared his urge was reinforced by observing the students at KUA and Dartmouth flinging around the cherry can lids. The combination of his theory and his inventive entrepreneurial spirit led Bill Robes to start thinking about making and

5. Malafronte, *The Complete Book of Frisbee*, page 52.

marketing a plastic version of the cherry can lid. These thoughts paralleled the thinking of Fred Morrison and Warren Franscioni far across the continent on the West Coast.

Robes put his idea into action during the very early 1950s. First, he painted a cherry can lid to be a prototype for what a plastic version might look like. He included the words "Space Saucer" in large block letters on the top of the lid, the name he chose for his device.

The differences between Bill Robes and Fred Morrison begin here. Fred and his partner, Warren Franscioni, were both Army Air Corp pilots who knew something about aerodynamics. They created several flying disc prototypes and tested each one for its flight characteristics, choosing the one that flew best. But Bill Robes already had what he felt flew best—his cherry can lid. The problem he thought he needed to solve was how to get a plastic version of his cherry can lid that was the exact shape and size of his painted prototype.

His solution was to put a square sheet of Boltaron plastic,[6] approximately three inches wider on each side than the diameter of his cherry can lid, into an oven and heat it until it was soft and pliable. He then used a wooden disc just slightly smaller in diameter than his cherry can lid to force the soft plastic sheet into the underside of the cherry can lid. While the plastic was cooling, he trimmed off the excess from around the edge of the cherry can. When cooled to room temperature, he pulled out the wooden disc and the result was a plastic version of the cherry can lid. That very first prototype plastic flying disc

6. Boltaron is a trade name for polyvinyl chloride, an early plastic that was available in the fifties.

that Bill Robes created was a virtual clone of the cherry can lid from which it was formed. It flew exactly like the painted "Space Saucer" cherry can lid![7]

The success that Bill Robes had with his inaugural prototype encouraged him to go on with his project. Using the mechanism from an old ringer-style washing machine tub, he invented a device whereby stepping on a pedal would push a wooden disc into a cavity he had created that was the same size as his cherry can lid prototype.

Bill's inaugural manufacturing process consisted of heating up a square sheet of Boltaron in a kitchen oven, placing it on the wooden disc, then pushing the pedal. The soft plastic oozed into the cavity and cooled

1953 Space Saucer prototype formed using a heated sheet of Boltaron plastic.

7. Bill Robes showed me his painted prototype cherry can lid and demonstrated how well it flew by playing toss and catch with me. He then showed me the very first prototype he made with that cherry can, and demonstrated how similar to the cherry can lid it flew. It was interesting to note that the concentric ribbing on the surface of the plastic disc matched exactly the concentric grooves on the underside of the cherry can lid. He gave me that first prototype Space Saucer and it became a treasured part of my collection. I got greedy and asked if he would give me the painted cherry can lid also. He said "Oh no, that's mine! I would never let that go!" —*Jim*

down into the exact shape of his original prototype. The name "Space Saucer" was molded onto the top of the plastic disc in large block letters. This was accomplished by inserting a die into the bottom of the cavity into which the soft plastic sheet was pushed. Robes also created an efficient method of trimming the excess plastic from each newly formed Space Saucer.

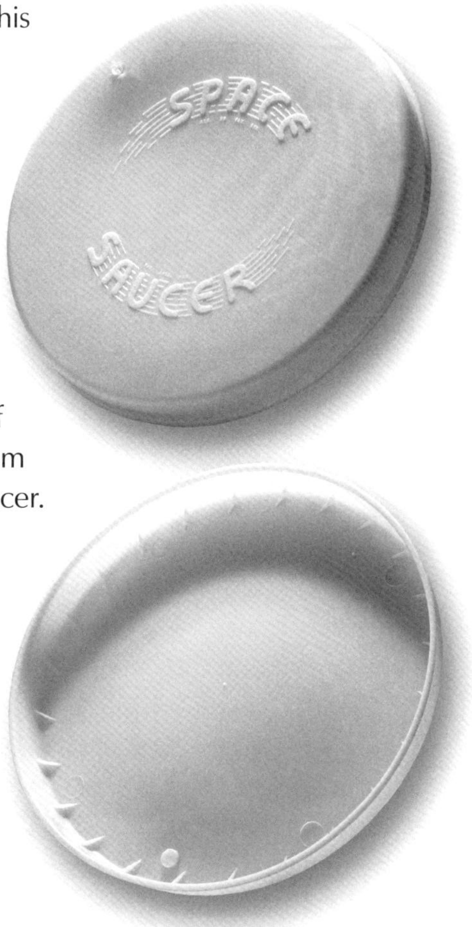

Front and back of a 1959 Space Saucer made using the plastic injection process.

This process was perfected by 1953. While it was certainly not a high-volume production, Bill Robes made enough Space Saucers to begin selling them to the Dartmouth students for 50 cents each. Cherry can and cookie tin lid flinging was already a very popular and somewhat organized activity on the Dartmouth campus at that time. The plastic Space Saucers offered many advantages over the tin lids in durability and safety, and soon were selling faster than Robes could make them on his device.

This early success led Robes to investigate the technology of producing Space Saucers by the plastic-injection molding process. By 1956 Robes had expanded his operation, selling Space Saucers not only on the Dartmouth campus, but to the Yale University College Bookstore and to other Ivy League schools as well.[8]

Now keep in mind, the origin and development of the Space Saucer disc on the East Coast was parallel to, but completely separate from, Fred Morrison and Warren Franscioni's development of the Flyin-Saucer on the West Coast.

Morrison and Franscioni were doing their best to market the Flyin-Saucer,[9] but their less-than-expected success led to Fred's discouragement, and they split up early in 1950. Warren Franscioni continued to market the original Flyin-Saucer for a short while before re-enlisting in the Air Force. Then in 1954 Fred Morrison started his own flying disc company called "American Trends." He created what is undeniably the most important disc in the evolution of the Frisbee culture, the Pluto Platter. It was a more attractive design than the original Flyin-Saucer, and it flew significantly better. However, Fred's marketing success wasn't any better. But one day, a critically important incident occurred that turns out to be *the* key factor in the origin of the Frisbee, the Frisbee culture, and disc sports. If this hadn't happened, you wouldn't be reading this book right now. This was the sperm that fertilized the egg.

One day in December 1956, as Fred was demonstrating Pluto Platter tossing and catching in a downtown Los Angeles parking

8. Bill Robes also showed me sales invoices from schools and retail stores in Michigan and Texas. —*Jim*

9. *Flat Flip Flies Straight* by Fred Morrison and Phil Kennedy covers the complete story in great detail.

lot, a stranger walked up to him and suggested that he show his Pluto Platters to Rich Knerr and Spud Melin, the owners and founders of the Wham-O Manufacturing Company.[10]

As it turned out, Rich and Spud had seen Fred demonstrate Platter tossing at the Pomona Fair earlier that year, and had already been mulling over the idea of marketing a flying saucer of their own. So when Fred made an appointment to meet with them and talk about his Pluto Platter, they were warmly receptive to the idea. An agreement between Fred Morrison and Wham-O was drawn up on January 23, 1957 (by chance, Fred's birthday). Wham-O took control of all production and marketing, leaving Fred to collect royalties from future sales.

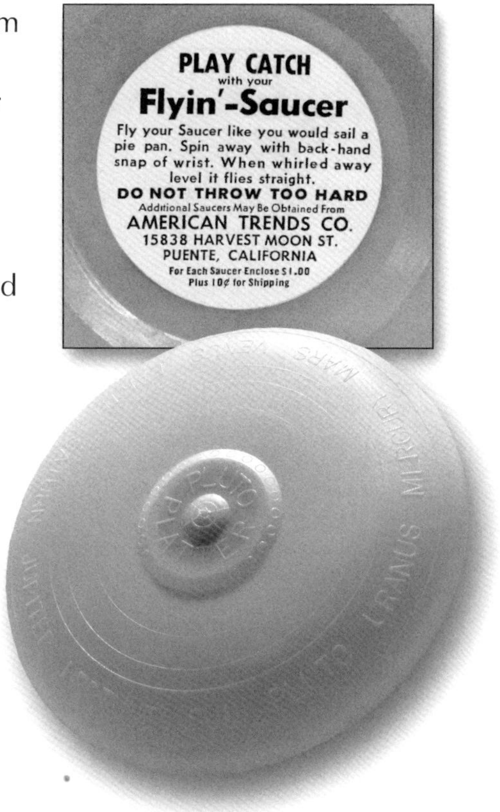

1955 American Trends Pluto Platter

However, the beginnings weren't as positive and smooth-sailing as either Fred Morrison or the Wham-O guys had hoped they would be. Sales of the Pluto Platter were not overly brisk. Several months later, Rich and Spud even created a companion

10. Morrison & Kennedy, *Flat Flip Flies Straight,* page 106.

to the Pluto Platter. It was a bigger disc named the "Sailing Satellite," but that didn't do much to spark sales. Flying discs just didn't catch the public's fancy in 1957 despite Wham-O's best attempts to promote it.

It was at this point that two important events occurred that led Wham-O to make a major decision that turned out to be what made "Frisbee" the household word that is today.

One event was the May 13, 1957 *Sports Illustrated* article mentioned in Chapter One.[11] This article specifically mentions:

> At Princeton, the air has been filled lately with flying objects, every one of which can be identified as a Pluto Platter made by Wham-O. The undergraduates ignore the official name, though, and call the curious gadgets Frisbees.[12]

No reference is made in the article to where the "Frisbee" name came from, just that that was the name the students were calling the recently introduced Pluto Platters.

There are two good reasons that make us believe that Rich Knerr and Spud Melin would have read this *Sports Illustrated* article. One, they were both avid sportsmen of the type that would be likely to read *Sports Illustrated*; and two, one of their business practices at that time was to collect every newspaper and magazine article about Wham-O products that they could find. I've seen some of the huge scrapbooks stuffed with these articles, and would find it hard to believe that they would have overlooked this popular one.

---

11. *Sports Illustrated,* May 13, 1957, page 22.

12. *Ibid.,* 22.

The other event that occurred during the spring of 1957 was that Rich Knerr took a business trip to the East Coast. This trip included visits to college campuses, where Rich may have observed students engaging in disc-flinging activities. Some students were still using the classic tin lids, but some were using the Space Saucers sold by Bill Robes, and some were using Wham-O's relatively new Pluto Platters. It's possible that Rich may have noticed that regardless of what brand or type of flying disc they were using, the students usually referred to them by the term "frizby," or any of the other spelling variations occasionally seen in print back in those days: "frisbie," "frisby," "frisbee," or whatever.[13] It is not known if Rich Knerr's trip East was in response to the number of newspaper and magazine articles he had read, or if it was an independently planned business trip. Regardless of the details, the bottom line was that the owners of Wham-O were fully apprised of the fact that their Pluto Platters were being called "Frisbees."

A critical part of marketing an item is brand-name recognition. Rich Knerr and Spud Melin were well aware of that principle and came to a quick and smart conclusion. Since flying disc products currently on the market were already being referred to as "Frisbees," why not try to boost sales by adopting that term for their disc? They successfully registered "Frisbee" as the trademark for Wham-O brand flying discs, and it became the official name for the Pluto Platter as well as all of their other discs to come.

Still, at that time, the percentage of the population engaging in Frisbee activity was quite small, and even with the name "Frisbee," sales of Pluto Platters were not brisk.

13. From a personal interview with Rich Knerr in February of 1980.

But Rich and Spud were not discouraged by the meager disc sales, because just as the first Frisbee-branded Pluto Platters hit the market in 1958, Wham-O hit the jackpot with the Hula Hoop—a hot new fad that instantly took the country by storm. In today's terminology, the Hula Hoop went viral. Virtually overnight it seemed everyone had to have a Hula Hoop. Rock & roll radio stations organized Hula Hoop contests; Woolworth five-and-dime stores had Hula Hoop experts doing demos in front of each of their outlets. Hula Hoops were selling like proverbial hotcakes—which strained Wham-O's production capacity to its limit. The situation almost resulted in the demise of the Frisbee.

Wham-O owners Spud Melin and Rich Knerr must have jumped for joy at the overnight success of the Hula Hoop.

Wham-O cut back on production of their Pluto Platter Frisbee, and eliminated their big Sailing Satellites completely. Wham-O had even contemplated dropping the Frisbee products from their line altogether, but the Hula Hoop fad had a dramatic, unplanned side effect. At the pinnacle of Hula Hoop sales, retail stores all over the country clamored for as many hoops as they could get their hands on. Sales reps had a field day. Instead of having to depend on cold-calls to generate outlets for Wham-O products, they were besieged with calls from anxious retailers not wanting to be left out of the Hula Hoop craze.

Almost overnight the number of outlets for Wham-O products grew geometrically. Sales reps were authorized to offer free shipping on orders of Wham-O's products if a customer spent over a specified amount. Since Hula Hoops were in short supply, Wham-O set a maximum number that each retailer was allowed to purchase per order...which just so happened to be under the minimum amount that needed to be spent for free shipping. Therefore, sales reps told their customers that if they bought a small number of Frisbee items, they would qualify for free shipping and save a lot of money. This sales promotion gained Wham-O huge market penetration for their new Frisbee products. Frisbees were placed on shelves in retail outlets all over the country, resulting in valuable exposure that ordinarily would have cost large sums of money for marketing and advertising programs. Then, when the Hula Hoop craze tanked almost as suddenly as it had soared, retailers began to contact their Wham-O sales reps and ask for "more of that Frisbee item," which turned out to be a slow but steady seller. This led Wham-O to abandon thoughts of dropping the Frisbee from their line of products and to push on with its marketing.[14]

Another key event that occurred at about the same time that Wham-O began its association with Fred Morrison was that Dick Warden, an avid cross-country skier, enrolled at Dartmouth.

---

14. This information was gathered during a 1980 personal interview with Dick Gillespie, who was the director of Research and Development for Wham-O Manufacturing Company during the time when the Hula Hoop's popularity put Wham-O on the map.

These two events seem totally unrelated. But Dartmouth College at that time was a hotbed of the Ivy League flying disc fad…the very place where Bill Robes, the ski-jumping coach, was hawking his Space Saucers. Bill met Dick and tried to recruit him for the Dartmouth Ski Jumping Team. This brought Dick into direct contact with Space Saucer activities, in which he remembers participating during his years at Dartmouth.[15] Like Fred Morrison's deal with Wham-O, the Dick Warden/Dartmouth College matchup is another of those fortuitous events that is responsible for the origin of today's Frisbee culture.

Around this same time, because the Frisbee was being marketed in retail stores all over the country, a friend of Dick Warden by the name of Jake Healy bought a Pluto Platter. Jake buying his Pluto Platter led to the creation of *the* "event" to which all organized Frisbee activities of today can trace their origin. That is a pretty big claim, but the facts will soon be presented to prove it.

The pre-plastic activities of the 1940s had developed into a relatively active fad on several college campuses by the early fifties, culminating with Dartmouth's big "International Frizby Match" in 1954. Ironically, this relatively well-developed and organized disc flying activity on the Dartmouth campus started to die out just as sales of plastic flying discs began to boom. The lid-flipping students finished their college days and moved on to graduate schools, jobs, and family responsibilities. No doubt some of them had bought their new-fangled plastic Space Saucers at the Dartmouth campus bookstore and packed

15. This information was gathered during a personal interview with Dick Warden at the 50th annual IFT in July of 2008.

them when they left. Later, in 1957, others remembered their college lid flinging when Wham-O's Pluto Platter hit the market, and perhaps bought one out of fond nostalgia. But the bottom line was that these early activities faded out of existence for the most part, and were only discovered to have happened when the historians of the current Frisbee culture started documenting Frisbee activity and researching where it all came from.

A very few of these early disc-flying activities persisted long enough in their own isolated spheres of activity so that they were still around when today's Frisbee culture was born. They became a part of the foundation from which the Frisbee culture began to evolve, each lending their own particular nuance and flavor to the mix.

The Frisbee Culture Catches On!

EARLIER, WE ESTABLISHED that plastic flying discs began to hit the market by the late '40s. In 1958, Wham-O's marketing efforts, fueled by the huge, instant success of the Hula Hoop, led to the Pluto Platter Frisbee being sold in stores all over the United States and Canada. This resulted in a large increase in the number of people who were exposed to flying discs.

On the underside of the Pluto Platter the phrase "Play Catch — Invent Games" was engraved in bold lettering. Every subsequent Frisbee model that Wham-O created and sold until 1975 also had that phrase molded into each disc. The people who bought

These immortal words were coined by Lu Morrison in 1954 for the American Trends Pluto Platter.

those discs enthusiastically complied: they played catch and invented games—all kinds of games and activities. In fact, they really didn't need to be encouraged to do so. The people who had played with tin lids and pie pans before plastic discs came along had created games on their own. The plastic era simply made this phenomenon more widespread.

Despite the growing number of people involved in flying disc activities prior to 1968, there still was no cohesive Frisbee culture, and really no widely recognized disc sports per se. However, many isolated pockets of Frisbee activity had sprouted up all over the country, ranging from casual tossing and catching to well-organized games and contests such as the annual International Frisbee Tournament (IFT) that will soon be discussed.

These isolated groups of Frisbee players were largely unaware of one another. Players who organized events communicated their activities via word of mouth and local news media. But John Doe over in the next county never heard anything about that activity. Even in big cities with good local news coverage, people rarely heard about organized Frisbee activities going on right under their noses, much less about such activities in other towns and states.

Perhaps the most significant example of this phenomenon of regionally isolated Frisbee play is the Guts game that was started in the Upper Peninsula of Michigan in 1958.

Jake Healy and three of his siblings, "Boots" Bob, Tim, and Pete came from a close-knit family who seemed to know how to mix fun, adventure, and celebration with the business of life in proper proportions. Their roots are in the Houghton-Escanaba-Eagle Harbor area of Michigan's Upper Peninsula.

Among their ways to have fun and celebrate, the Healy family held picnics and parties that included eating food, consuming beer, and engaging in a variety of outdoor games, one of which was golf. Some of these picnics and celebrations were tied to special events like weddings, birthdays, graduations, and holidays such as the Fourth of July. The Healys often invited friends and business associates to join them in their festivities.

Sometime during the spring of 1958, while attending law school at the University of Michigan in Ann Arbor, Jake Healy noticed something new happening on campus: Frisbee flinging. Jake thought it looked like fun and joined in, buying himself a Pluto Platter. Serendipity of the highest order! You will see....

At Jake's wedding reception on June 14, 1958 in Houghton, Michigan, there were several Pluto Platters on hand. Part of the wedding reception festivities included tossing around the Pluto Platters, each of which had "Play Catch – Invent Games" on their underside. Jake Healy, his brothers, and their guests fully obeyed that now legendary dictum, and had lots of fun playing catch and inventing games with their Frisbees.

In one game they came up with on that memorable wedding day the players stood approximately fifteen yards apart, zinging the Pluto Platter back and forth, testing their opponent's ability to catch the thing. For the next four days, before Jake left on his honeymoon, the Healy brothers played their new game often, codifying the basic rules, and naming the game "Guts."

Later that year in Escanaba, Michigan, at a Labor Day picnic and birthday party for Tim Healy, three of the Healy brothers, Tim, Pete, and "Boots" Bob, along with their cousin Jim Boggio and good friend Dick Warden, teamed up and challenged teams of other guests to some Guts matches. No one could beat the Healy brothers' team at their game and they were declared the champions of the celebration.[1]

When 1959 rolled around, the Healy family held a Fourth of July picnic. The Frisbee fun of the Labor Day/birthday party celebration of the previous year was keenly remembered, and repeated—Guts matches and all. Other new Frisbee activities were a significant component of this picnic. They held an accuracy contest consisting of trying to throw a Frisbee through an old tire hanging by a rope from a tree. They also had a distance throwing contest. The competition was organized into several age divisions for the kids: under 6, under 10, and under 15...and one adult division.[2] The Healy brothers and Dick Warden again teamed up for the Guts matches, this time including Jake Healy as a team member. Taking on all challengers, they again prevailed.

As they planned another Fourth of July picnic the next summer, the Healy brothers were aware of the new tradition of Frisbee competition they had spawned. Therefore, the plans for the 1960 picnic included having teams ready to compete in a Guts Frisbee tournament. They also repeated the accuracy and distance contests that year. The Healy brothers and Dick Warden again teamed up, and once again, won it all. They became known as the "North Central Guts Frisbee Team" and had gained quite a reputation for their Guts Frisbee prowess.

---

1. In retrospect, as the Healy brothers' subsequent Frisbee activities evolved, this gathering and Guts competition would go down as the first annual "International Frisbee Tournament," even though at the time it occurred, they didn't know it was going to be called that retroactively.

2. The information about the Healy family's early involvement with Frisbee came from a personal interview that Joe Feidt conducted with Jake Healy in October of 2009.

Somewhere between 1960 and 1963, the Frisbee contests and the Guts competitions became the primary focus of the annual Healy family's Fourth of July celebration. The Healy brothers made their picnic an open house to anyone who wanted to come and compete in the Frisbee contests, and began to call it the "International Frisbee Tournament."

This annual "IFT" event began to take on a specific persona and format, where fun, beer, and merriment were the foremost requirements. They derived a great deal of enjoyment out of the event by promoting it as a quasi-"seriously competitive" tournament, spoofing collegiate and professional football, basketball, and baseball competition. They wrote up news releases, heavy on the tongue-in-cheek, touting a number of fictitious characters who purportedly possessed finely honed and highly regarded Frisbee skills. The primary fictional character was "Harvey J. Kukuk" as their beloved tournament director. They created the "International Frisbee Association" with head offices in Minneapolis, Minnesota to further enhance the satirical side of their annual event. The head of this association was none other than the legendary Harvey J. Kukuk himself.

It is interesting to note that some of the character and trappings that evolved during these early IFT years are quite similar to the antics and lore of the early tin lid "Frizby" game" played at Dartmouth College during the 1950s.

Remember that Dick Warden, the Healy brothers' extremely close friend and teammate from the very beginning, was a student at Dartmouth College during that Frizby period of time. While at Dartmouth, Dick Warden was aware of and played the Frizby game that was a part of the Dartmouth campus lore. The game developed into cult-like proportions culminating in the big "International Frizby Match" of November 1954.[3] It was at this period of time that Bill Robes had started to market his Space Saucer at Dartmouth and other college campuses. As a matter of fact, a newspaper article chronicling the International Frizby Match of 1954 specifically stated that the participants of this match "eschewed" the new-fangled plastic flying saucers seen flying about the campus, and chose to use the traditional tin lid for the competition.

Dick does not remember specifically how much influence he may have had on the formulation of the early Guts game and the matches they had, but the attributes and format of the evolving Guts game and IFT event were amazingly similar to the Frizby game played earlier on the campus of Dartmouth College.

The Frizby game contested at the 1954 International Frizby Match was described as a gentleman's game that was self-refereed. Similarly, Guts participants of the annual IFT still take pride in the fact that they need no referees.

An important rule of Dartmouth's International Frizby Match was that competitors were expected to keep a container of their favorite spirits at their foot during the match. The Guts game of the IFT developed a rule called "Addendum 69b" which stated that all players must have a can of beer with them at all times during a game. In each case, these rules were playful and were not strictly enforced, nor were penalties assessed for infractions of the rule.

---

3. Malafronte, *The Complete Book of Frisbee*, pages 51–55.

Coincidence? Perhaps, but it is easier to believe that when the Healy brothers were playing their Guts game with Dick Warden as a teammate, Dick may have suggested some ideas from the Friszby game he had played while a student at Dartmouth. Neither Dick Warden nor Jake Healy remember the specific details about the early formulation of the Guts game other than they put it together on that wedding day, had a lot of fun with it, and continued playing it from that point on. Keep in mind that Dick Warden was at Jake Healy's wedding reception. He was fresh out of Dartmouth and his Frizby playing days. It is certainly likely that he had a hand in making suggestions about how the game could be played as it came into being that day. Furthermore, Dick continued to be part and parcel of the original Guts get-togethers during which the format for the Guts matches kept evolving.

Despite the fact that Jake and Dick don't recall all of the details about the origin of their Guts game, Jake remembers that he always won the distance throwing contest at the annual event, and that his brother Bob usually won the accuracy contest, with brother Tim winning it some of the time.

This creative fun and merriment was rolling along in 1964 when the Healy brothers, disguised as Harvey J. Kukuk and the International Frisbee Association, made their first contact with Wham-O about their annual IFT. After Fred Morrison's creation of the Pluto Platter in 1954, and making his deal with Wham-O in 1957, this occurrence is the third critical juncture responsible for today's cohesive Frisbee culture.

In 1964, Wham-O hired Ed Headrick to help with the general marketing of their products. Ed was the consummate entrepreneur as well as an inventor. From Ed's perspective Wham-O, with all their gadgets and fun things to play with, looked like a great place to work. It is said that when Ed went there seeking a job, there were no job openings at the time, but he cajoled Rich Knerr and Spud Melin, the co-owners of Wham-O, by telling them he would work for free the first month. If they liked what they saw, they could keep him on and start paying him.

If that story is true, Rich and Spud apparently liked what they saw in Ed Headrick, because he did stay on with them, eventually becoming a vice-president and the man in charge of the day-to-day operations.

Ed Headrick joined Wham-O in 1964

When Ed Headrick joined Wham-O, the company was in the process of evaluating which new products and ideas might be worthy to market, and which of their slower-moving items might be dropped from their line to make room for new products. The "Turbo Tube" was one of the casualties at this time. The Turbo Tube was similar to the Frisbee in that it could be sailed through the air in the very same toss-and-catch manner that was the hallmark of the Frisbee disc. Its flight characteristics

were similar to the Frisbee, and were just as intriguing.[4] But it was determined that the sales volume and market predictions did not merit its continuation.

The relatively slow-selling Frisbee discs were also being considered for retirement for the same reasons. But before the final decision was made whether or not to drop the Frisbee products, the Healy brothers and Wham-O made contact with each other. Wham-O learned about their big annual International Frisbee Tournament and heard about the International Frisbee Association. This caught the ear of Ed Headrick, who began corresponding with the Healy brothers about their Frisbee activities. Ed began to wonder about the potential future sales volume of the Frisbee discs and started to think about new ways that the items could be marketed. This turned out to be a very important turn of events. Ed used

4. I have played with a Wham-O Turbo Tube, and can attest to the fact that it is indeed quite similar to a Frisbee in many aspects of its flight characteristics and capacity for fun and games. The "Play Catch—Invent Games" concept of the Frisbee applied to the Turbo Tube in the very same manner. I even experimented with playing Double Disc Court and Disc Golf with Turbo Tubes, and was amazed at how interchangeable they were for those activities! —*Jim*

FRISBEE!
8th Annual International
Frisbee Tournament
JULY 4, 1965
2:00 O'CLOCK P.M.
Eagle Harbor Ballyard
EAGLE HARBOR, MICHIGAN
Wholesome Outdoor Entertainment for All Ages
Thumb Sucking - Beer Drinking - Queens in Attendance
MAIN EVENT:
GUTS FRISBEE Contest
for Julius Nachazel International Team Trophy
Also Distance & Accuracy Contests
POMP - PRIZES
PAGEANTRY

the information about the annual IFT and the International Frisbee Association to convince Spud and Rich that they shouldn't give up on the Frisbee products just yet, that he had some ideas that they should try first.

One of the important things that Ed did at this point was to retool the Pluto Platter mold into the "Official Pro Model" Frisbee. In exchange for establishing the Pro Model Frisbee as the official disc for the annual International Frisbee Tournament, Wham-O offered to help sponsor the IFT event and keep the Healy brothers supplied with Pro Models to use at the tournament.

The discussion about dropping the Frisbee from Wham-O's product line ceased abruptly—and never came up again. Support from Wham-O enhanced the Healy brothers' enthusiasm for their fun event, and the IFT started to grow significantly. The growth of the IFT in turn started to increase the popularity and sales of Wham-O Frisbees. This in turn led Wham-O to increase promotional efforts for the IFT, which in turn further increased the growth of the event.

The Pluto Platter mold was retooled in the fall of 1964 to create the new Official Pro Model

This escalating symbiotic relationship between Wham-O and the IFT continued for a number of years, and was the ipso facto origin of today's worldwide Frisbee culture. All of the organized disc sports of today can trace their lineage back to Wham-O's decision to continue producing the Frisbee product line, to develop the Pro Model, and to support and help build up the IFT.

Ed Headrick first attended the IFT in 1968. His presence and participation further increased his enthusiasm for all things Frisbee, and fueled his ideas on how to promote sales of Frisbees. Perhaps the very most significant decision that Ed Headrick made at this time was to adopt the Healy brothers' fictional International Frisbee Association (IFA) and turn it into a promotional tool for Wham-O. Ed picked up on the Healy brothers' penchant for fun and their ongoing satire of organized sports, and he incorporated it into Wham-O's version of the IFA. Ed even adopted the fictional Harvey J. Kukuk, designating him the director of the International Frisbee Association.

The most critically important aspect about this decision to create a quasi-real International Frisbee Association was Ed's idea to create the *IFA Newsletter*. This newsletter was intended to hype the enthusiasm for Frisbee play in general, and to inform its readers of Frisbee happenings around the world. It was sent out to anyone who became a member of the IFA. Membership in the IFA was offered on the packaging of each Frisbee sold. For 50¢ anyone could become a lifetime member of the IFA and receive its newsletter absolutely free. It was a great deal, and thousands of Frisbee players from all over the U.S. and Canada took advantage of this offer. A primary focus of the *IFA Newsletter* was to promote and disseminate

©1967 **INTERNATIONAL FRISBEE® ASSOCIATION** 2900 Rowena Avenue
Los Angeles, California 90039

I would like to become a member of the International Frisbee® Association. Please send me my official IFA membership card, IFA membership certificate, FRISBEE® manual, proficiency qualification form and the FRISBEE® Newsletter as fast as you can. i have enclosed a 50¢ membership fee (no stamps, please), which qualifies me as a FRISBEE® Novice and which also covers handling and mailing costs.

NAME__________ AGE____ SEX____
(Please Print)

ADDRESS__________
(Number) (Street)

____
(City) (State) (Zip)

Which model FRISBEE® do you own?

REGULAR__ PROFESSIONAL__ MASTER TOURNAMENT__ MINI-FRISBEE®__

The proficiency qualification form will give you the requirements necessary to establish your individual classification under IFA world-wide standards — Amateur, Expert, or Master.

information about the annual IFT on the Upper Peninsula of Michigan.

The advent of the *IFA Newsletter* in 1968 marks the beginning of a five-year period during which Frisbee enthusiasts from all over began to learn about one another for the very first time, commencing the evolution of a cohesive and worldwide Frisbee culture. This period from 1968–1973 was crucially important and can be designated as the gestation period that culminated in the 1973 IFT. The 1973 IFT was a special happening...with avid players meeting other avid players and enthusiastically exchanging ideas. The 1973 IFT can be said to be the actual birth date of disc sports as we know them today.

Until the Wham-O IFA and its newsletter began in 1968, virtually all the people actively playing Frisbee thought that they and their friends were the only ones who were enthusiastic enough to spend so much time and effort playing with flying discs. People playing throw-and-catch games with a Frisbee in

IFA NEWSLETTER

INTERNATIONAL FRISBEE ASSOCIATION

VOLUME I, NUMBER 1 2900 Rowena Avenue, Los Angeles, California 90039

FOR THE GOOD OF THE SPORT

Willingness of FRISBEE players throughout the world to sacrifice their freedom to practice FRISBEE in the way of their choosing "for the sake of the sport" has resulted in the formation of the International Frisbee Association. Headquartered in Los Angeles, the IFA will serve as a central communications forum to strengthen the bonds among FRISBEE players everywhere.

IFA Executive Director Robert Werden said considerable soul-searching preceded formation of the international body. "It is regrettable that FRISBEE has attained such worldwide popularity that it is necessary to confine the spirit of freedom which has long marked the FRISBEE player within the strictures of an organization, no matter how well-intentioned," Werden said.

"However, the clamor by FRISBEE players from many nations to achieve status within the Olympic Games has necessitated the development of a body which would set standards of proficiency, rules and regulations."

Werden pointed out that during the past score of years FRISBEE has progressed from the scaling of pie tins by small groups to the skillful spinning projection of the aerodynamically-designed plastic disk used by thousands of players today.

The IFA Board of Governors already has established standards of proficiency for the four categories of FRISBEE player — novice, amateur, expert and master — and is reviewing suggestions from enthusiasts throughout the world for the formation of rules and regulations.

"Once these have been compiled into a standardized form for worldwide usage," he said, "they will be submitted to the IFA membership for ratification.

"We are confident that both the standards of proficiency, rules and regulations will preserve every FRISBEE player's inalienable right — to move up in the ranks of classification, limited only by his own ability."

Werden said the IFA Board of Governors is convinced that as soon as the criteria for international competition have been established by the membership, an effective presentation can be made to the International Olympic Committee.

"Meanwhile," he added, "IFA will bring about lend-lease of FRISBEE techniques and theories among the players of every nation in the Free World."

Applications for membership are now being processed by the IFA, headquartered at 2900 Rowena Avenue, Los Angeles, California 90039.

PROFICIENCY STANDARDS ESTABLISHED BY IFA

Standards of Proficiency as an international guide for all FRISBEE players have been developed by the IFA Board of Governors and Charter members. These are now being reviewed for final amendments and ratification.

Within the IFA there will be four classifications of members — Novice, Amateur, Expert and Master. A qualification form will be sent to each member who considers himself qualified to move up in classification. Promotion in category will be certified by the Board of Governors upon completion of the duly-executed, duly-witnessed form.

IFA has also established three categories for annual membership dues.

These are as follows:

All proficiency classifications for those under 12 years of age, $1.00 per year. IFA Newsletter not included.

All proficiency classifications for those between 12 and 18 years of age, $1.50 per year. IFA Newsletter not included.

All proficiency classifications for those 18 years of age and older, $3.00 per year. IFA Newsletter included.
(IFA Newsletter subscription price, $1.00 per year)

IFA certification fees are:

Amateur — $2.00. Applicant receives amateur identification/membership card and certificate.

Expert — $5.00. Applicant receives expert identification/membership card, certificate, IFA Expert blazer patch, special personal FRISBEE.

Master — $10.00. Applicant receives gold lifetime membership card, certificate, IFA Master blazer patch and personalized Master FRISBEE with carrying case.

All FRISBEE players who have any questions regarding any facet of the IFA are invited to direct their inquiries to the Executive Director at the IFA headquarters.

WHENCE FRISBEE?

Just who shot the first FRISBEE into the air will probably remain a mystery forever. Some say its pre-history encompasses the athletes of the Olympics of 776 B.C. who eventually traded their crude FRISBEEs in for the discus.

Others claim that FRISBEE did indeed originate in the cradle of civilization but was far from being a game. Instead they reveal that the ingenious Greeks discovered that they could sever their adversaries by scaling their shields, once spear supplies ran out.

In the modern epoch, the well-spring of FRISBEE has been credited to various universities with Princeton, Dartmouth, Yale and Harvard among those most frequently mentioned. Yale claims FRISBEE began there over a century ago. Their historian has produced documentation to prove the sport originated in 1827 by Yaleman Elihu Frisbee who, in protest against compulsory chapel, scaled a collection plate 200 feet across the Yale campus. This noble act began a craze on the Yale scene which lasted until the Great Collection Plate Shortage of 1873. During the following decades, experimentation for a substitute was vigorously carried out with everything from pizza trays to manhole covers being tried.

IFA historians place the beginning of the modern FRISBEE era at approximately 20 years ago, just after World War II, when the clientele of the Frisbee Baking Company of Bridgeport, Connecticut, discovered that the tin plates which held Mother Frisbee's pies were excellent for scaling. An IFA member in Connecticut disclosed that his investigation showed that the company lost 5,000 plates during the height of the pie-plate-pitching fad.

Thus the venerated name was born. But the final perfection in aerodynamics was attained some 13 years ago by a Mr. Fred Morrison, in San Fernando, California, who, and such quirks of irony dot history's pages, developed a plastic saucer originally intended to be a children's toy. How could he have foreseen the benefits his inventiveness would bring to the international sporting world?

Today Mr. Morrison, an honored member of IFA's Board of Governors, and Wham-O Manufacturing Company, who took his now sacrosanct prototype and made the world FRISBEE conscious, work hand in hand in a never-ending effort to refine and improve the FRISBEE.

IFA

STATEMENT OF PURPOSES

Whereas the sport of FRISBEE has progressed during the past two decades from the use of pie tins by a small group of devotees to the skillful spinning projection of aerodynamically-designed plastic disks by thousands of practitioners of FRISBEE throughout the world, now therefore, do we members of the International Frisbee Association set forth and ordain the following as our Statement of Purposes in promulgating the sport of FRISBEE to its ultimate destiny.

1. *Consequent to the development of FRISBEE and the refining of individual techniques and forms of competition, there has been an increased demand for communications among the world's FRISBEE players. The IFA will serve as focal point of worldwide FRISBEE communications, linking the FRISBEE players of every continent who have the common bond of enthusiasm, and disseminating news of FRISBEE to all IFA members.*

2. *As in life's pursuits, the aim to excel should be uppermost in the goals of all IFA members. Self-betterment is to be strongly encouraged among individual IFA members prior to their participation in competitive team play.*

3. *To help every FRISBEE player to judge his own skill, the IFA will establish standards of proficiency, accomplishment and excellence.*

4. *Competitive instinct and pride of personal achievement, so vital to the IFA member, shall be encouraged through the individual's ability to direct his own progress, limited only by his own ability to master the various standards of proficiency which mark the FRISBEE player's classification — Novice, Amateur, Expert and Master.*

5. *Recognizing that indiyidual FRISBEE enthusiasts throughout the world have in many instances developed certain forms of activity, accomplishment and competition, the IFA will, through its membership, set forth rules and regulations covering any and all forms of IFA-sanctioned FRISBEE competition. No other governing body in athletics, including the International Olympic Committee and Amateur Athletic Union, can take precedence over the IFA in the establishment of such rules and regulations.*

6. *The IFA and each IFA member will at all times strive to establish increased rapport and camaraderie among all IFA members through the exchange of ideas for improvement and participation in the development of rewarding programs for both group and individual participation.*

their back yard or at a public park didn't capture the attention of the news media. And there was no YouTube or Internet. The few public Frisbee events that did occur prior to 1968 were reported locally at best...if they were reported at all.

But when they began reading the *IFA Newsletter,* Frisbee enthusiasts discovered that many other disc tossers were out there, and perhaps were just as enthusiastic about Frisbee as they were! For the very first time there was a real link and a line of communication between Frisbee players everywhere.

Among a variety of Frisbee tidbits, these new *IFA Newsletter* readers learned about the game of Guts and the annual IFT event. Some of them formed teams and traveled to the IFT to try their hand at competing. Because of this, 1968 is the year in which the IFT event began to grow in geometric proportions. Guys like John Connelly, Tom Cleworth, Alan Blake, Dave Bradshaw, and Stan Korth from the Highland Avenue area of Wilmette, Illinois had been playing Frisbee for a number of years, developing excellent throwing and catching skills. They read about the IFT and thought that since they were absolutely the very best Frisbee players in their local area, they could go to the IFT as a team and kick butt! And they certainly did! They named their team the "Highland Avenue Aces," traveled to the IFT in 1970, and almost conquered the veteran IFT powerhouse "Foul Five" team to take second place in their very first appearance at the tournament. Realizing that being the best in the Chicago area wasn't good enough, they went home and practiced their newly acquired game. The Highland Avenue Aces returned and subsequently reeled off three IFT Championships in a row (1971 through 1973), and for good measure, added a runner-up finish in 1974!

The very same process occurred with John Sappington, Scott Dickson, Vaughn Frick, John and Jo Cahow, and others from the Ann Arbor, Michigan area. These Frisbee lovers had also gained the reputation of being the very best Frisbee players in their local area, and they also thought that they could go up to the IFT and show everyone who was boss. They called their team the "Humbly Magnificent Champions of the Universe," a deserved name, at least in comparison to other Frisbee players from the Ann Arbor area at the time. Although they didn't quite achieve the level of success at the IFT as the Highland Avenue Aces did, they were always a major competitive force and a team to be reckoned with, finishing in second place twice.

Ditto with the Guys from Berkeley! Steve Gottlieb, Chuck Pitt, Roger Barret, Dave Book, Chuck Shultz, Victor Malafronte, John Weyand, Steve Sewell, Bob May, and Jay Shelton were some of the powerhouse Frisbee players centered around the University of California at Berkeley from 1967–1973. These guys called themselves the "Berkeley Frisbee Group," or "BFG" for short. When they read about the IFT and its Guts competition, they too thought along the lines of "How can we lose? Nobody is better than we are at Frisbee playing!" And that was totally true in their local Berkeley area. They were a significant presence at the IFT during that 1968 to 1973 period. Steve Sewell and Jay Shelton, early de facto leaders of the BFG, attended the 1968 and 1969 IFT and played with the "California Masters" team, leading them to victory in both years. Bob May, another mainstay of the BFG, traveled to the IFT in 1970 and joined the aforementioned Foul Five team, helping them win the 1970 title—nipping the upstart Highland Avenue Aces. In subsequent years the BFG came to the IFT with so many players that they formed two teams, and like their Humbly counterparts from Ann Arbor, they took second place honors twice.

This process of discovering the IFA and reading its newsletter occurred all over the country. Ardent Frisbee players formed teams, journeyed to the IFT and joined in on the fun and competition. Each of these groups brought with them their own particular flavor of Frisbee activities, and gladly exchanged ideas and lore with one another. The Highland Avenue Aces from Chicago, the Humblies from Ann Arbor, and the Berkeley Frisbee Group all met, and along with many other Frisbee enthusiasts, became good friends as well as Guts Frisbee rivals. They exchanged ideas and learned new activities from one another which they brought home to their local groups, who further spread the word about Frisbee events. Many of them started up Guts and Frisbee events in their own local area. This brought legions of newcomers to Frisbee activities, some of whom became IFA members and who also started going to the IFT. They became part of the fast-escalating cycle of Frisbee awareness and growth during the early 1970s. From 1968 to 1973, Frisbee grew from being a relatively unknown activity played by isolated groups of people who didn't know of each other's existence, to a huge national culture with the *IFA Newsletter* as its bible and the IFT as its Mecca.

CHAPTER 4

A CHAIN OF EVENTS

The Rise of the Frisbee Culture

SO FAR WE'VE DESCRIBED the significant events that led to the beginning of a Frisbee culture. Without all of those events happening in the order and manner that they did, the plastic flying disc might not have come into existence when it did, much less reached the popularity that enabled the emergence of the IFA and its newsletter!

We can only conjecture how long it might have been before tin lid recreational activities caught on, at which time an entirely different set of factors would have occurred, causing plastic discs, disc sports, and Disc Golf to emerge. The only thing we can be sure about is that the outcome would be entirely different from how things have turned out today.

Fortunately, things *did* transpire as they did. Ed Headrick's response to the Healy brothers' IFT event *did* save the Frisbee, and things *did* progress from there. The following extremely significant people who had become deeply involved with their Frisbee activity *were* eventually brought together by the *IFA Newsletter,* and disc sports, as we know them today, began to evolve.

One of these important Frisbee enthusiasts to be flushed out of obscurity by the *IFA Newsletter* was George Sappenfield. As a young guy of fourteen in 1960, he started tossing a Pluto Platter around with a neighbor in Fresno, California. He became fascinated with the flight of the Frisbee and it became one of his regular avenues of recreation.

During his summer break from college in 1965, nineteen-year-old George was working as a playground counselor for the Fresno Parks and Recreation Department. While he was playing golf with some friends on one of his afternoons off, it occurred to him that the kids on his playground could play the game of golf using Frisbees instead of a ball and set of clubs. His new "Frisbee Golf" game was a playground success. Upon his graduation from college in 1968, he became director of the Conejo Valley Recreation and Parks Department in Thousand Oaks, California, and incorporated Frisbee Golf and other Frisbee activities as part of his recreation program. He set up a course around one of the playground areas and set aside one day a week as "Frisbee Golf Day."

George's interest in Frisbee activities led him to discover the new *IFA Newsletter* which he responded to by contacting Wham-O to tell them about his Frisbee Golf game and a Frisbee Golf tournament he was planning to stage for his playground kids. Irv Lander, Director of Promotions at Wham-O, traveled to Thousand Oaks to further investigate George's idea of Frisbee Golf. Irv was somewhat new to Wham-O and had not been aware that Wham-O had previously heard about Frisbee Golf from a similar event that had taken place in 1965 in Newport Beach, California. Irv was quite fascinated with George's Frisbee activities, and he was further impressed with George's background and expertise in recreation in general. He felt that George could help him with a big promotional idea that he was working on, and hired George as a consultant for Wham-O. Irv asked George to help design and plan a National Junior Frisbee Championship event, which later became a huge annual promotion under the auspices of the IFA. George's efforts with this program introduced Frisbee activities to hundreds of thousands of young people all across the country.

George was also asked to help plan and set up a large promotional Frisbee event scheduled for November 2, 1969 at Brookside Park in Pasadena, California. This event was officially billed as the "California Meet," but became known as the "All Comers Meet," specifically because it was open to all who wanted to come and try their hand at a variety of Frisbee activities.

Along with the classic "guts," this important meet offered a variety of what were billed as "activity areas." These included: "distance," "accuracy," "style throwing and catching," and "free exercise." Because of George Sappenfield's input, with support from Irv Lander, a "9-hole Frisbee golf course" activity area was also included.

Although Wham-O promoted this event in the typically whimsical manner of the original IFT and the jargon of the *IFA Newsletter,* many players who answered the call were quite serious competitors. At stake was the prestige of being known as one of the best Frisbee players on the planet.

This All Comers Meet became an early forerunner of competitive disc sports. The guys from Berkeley, the BFG,

The long-awaited California meet has been scheduled for Sunday, November 2, 1969, starting at 10:00 a.m. at Brookside Park, Pasadena, California (see map on reverse).

All day - do your own thing and eat your own lunch.

Activity areas:

- 9-hole Frisbee golf course
- distance
- accuracy
- style throwing and catching
- guts
- free exercise

Who will be there:

- California Masters team
- World's distance champion
- Some of California's best Frisbee throwers
- Some of California's worst Frisbee throwers
- Someone to Frisbee with
- You

You can challenge anyone you like--or don't like.

Bring family, friends, food.

Frisbees will be supplied.

PLEASE RETURN ENCLOSED CARD IF YOU PLAN TO ATTEND

IFA
INTERNATIONAL FRISBEE® ASSOCIATION
P. O. Box 4
Alhambra, California 91802
(213) 285-2125

IFA invitation letter to the California ("All Comers") Meet held November 2, 1969

had also discovered the *IFA Newsletter,* and responded by contacting Wham-O about their activities. This led to some of them joining Ed Headrick in forming a Guts team to go to the 1968 IFT, as well as the 1969 All Comers event. Other than George Sappenfield himself, the BFG guys were the only participants at the meet who had really played Frisbee Golf before. Jay Shelton had discovered playing golf with a Frisbee while a student at Harvard University. When he came to Berkeley for graduate school in 1967, he met the other Berkeley Frisbee players and showed them the concept of Frisbee Golf, which became one of their regular activities as they evolved into the BFG. So when they came to the All Comers Meet, they were experienced Frisbee golfers, unlike many of the other attendees who had never even heard of Frisbee Golf, much less played the game before. With Jay Shelton leading the way, the BFG members dominated the golf game and were a good example for the other participants to see what Frisbee Golf was all about. Jay Shelton had the best score of the day, and was crowned the "Champion of the Frisbee Golf Activity."

The members of the Berkeley Frisbee Group were a creative bunch of Frisbee players, and introduced many new ideas to the concept of Frisbee playing. Led by Victor Malafronte and John "Dreamer" Weyand, they introduced many of the fancy trick throws and catches that helped inspire the later development of Freestyle competition. The Self-Caught Flight (SCF) events of "Throw, Run, and Catch" (TRC), and "Maximum Time Aloft" (MTA) were invented by BFG guru Roger Barrett, and were introduced to the Frisbee community at the IFT in the early '70s.

Also notable during the early '70s were brothers Mike and Bill Schneider, who traveled abroad several times to promote Frisbee activities. George Sappenfield accompanied them on one of their trips, bringing the full support of Wham-O's promotional efforts. These European tours of Frisbee play resulted in laying a solid foundation for the nascent European Frisbee culture.

The *IFA Newsletter* also brought ardent Frisbee player Ken Westerfield into communication with the developing Frisbee culture. In the Fall of 1973, the *IFA Newsletter* induced Ken to travel to the Berkeley campus for a visit with the BFG. Ken was residing in Toronto, Ontario at the time, itself a growing kernel of Frisbee play. Ken and his good friend Jim Kenner were the counterparts of Victor Malafronte and John "Dreamer" Weyand of the BFG. Ken's visit to Berkeley inspired an important exchange of Frisbee ideas and was another key catalyst to the growth of the burgeoning Frisbee culture. Ken and Jim organized the very first Freestyle for Pairs competition, an event held in conjunction with the third annual Canadian Open Frisbee Championships held on August 17–18, 1974. That Freestyle event kicked off the beginning of the sport of Freestyle as we know it today. But they didn't stop with Freestyle; they both also took an avid interest in Disc Golf. It was Ken and Jim's efforts that built the foundation for Disc Golf in Canada. They started with a Disc Golf event at the fourth annual Canadian Open Frisbee Championships in 1975, and were instrumental in getting the now-legendary Toronto Island Disc Golf course installed. They developed a steady program of Disc Golf competition at that Toronto Island course, and Jim Kenner went on to start the Discraft company.

Similarly, the IFA and its newsletter enticed Tom McCrann to leave his native New England and travel to the Palo Alto area of California seeking Frisbee play. He met the BFG players in 1973, and got involved in promoting Frisbee fun in a variety of ways, including persuading Stanford University to let him teach a course about Frisbee! Tom is also credited with introducing the Fastback Frisbee model as the disc to use for MTA competition. From the time of its introduction in 1973 until Tom demonstrated its superiority for MTA competition three years later, the Fastback Frisbee model was thought to be useless as a competitive flying disc. Because of its unobstructed flat topside that was perfect for printing messages, it was considered important only as a promotional tool. But that didn't deter Tom from experimenting with it and finding out that its unique flight characteristics were well suited for MTA.

A whopper of a catch by the *IFA Newsletter* was a guy named Dr. Stancil Johnson. In 1960, when he was a young man in medical school, he attended a picnic to which someone had brought a Wham-O Sailing Satellite.[1]

The Sailing Satellite was produced from mid-1957 to 1958

1. The Sailing Satellite was the only Wham-O flying disc that did not get marketed as a "Frisbee" brand flying disc. This was because it was created before Wham-O decided to start using the name "Frisbee" for their flying disc line. It was dropped in 1958—a victim of the big Hula Hoop boom.

It caught Stancil's attention in the same manner as the popcorn can lid had caught Fred Morrison's attention twenty-three years earlier. And Stancil's response was similar. He was fascinated with the Sailing Satellite, and tossed it back and forth all day long with any willing picnickers he could find. As the activities wound down and it was time for Stancil to leave, the host of the picnic told him that he had never seen anyone have as much fun as he did with that disc, and that he wanted Stancil to keep the Sailing Satellite and take it home with him.

That day marked the start of a lifelong passion and devotion to all things pertaining to Frisbee for Stancil. Then, in 1968, he saw the information about the IFA in the package of one of the Frisbee discs he bought, and decided to join the organization. As luck would have it, he happened to be in Southern California at the moment, so instead of mailing the membership form, he went directly to the IFA address in person to sign up. He met Robert Werdon, the first director of the new Wham-O IFA. Robert Werdon was impressed that Stancil had made the effort to show up in person, and they had a long chat about Frisbee and the current state of the art.

Among other things, Stancil found out about the upcoming annual IFT and decided he would attend the event. As more luck would have it, Stancil saw several people on the airplane who were carrying some Frisbee discs along with them. So Stancil asked them if they were going to Eagle Harbor for the IFT. The response from one of them was a gruffly uttered "Why else would we be going to that God-forsaken place!" It was none other than Ed Headrick himself, who was also making his first visit to the IFT to make good on his longstanding boast to the Healy brothers that he was the world's best Frisbee player.

Ed had told Bob Healy that he and his team could easily win the IFT. Ed and the Healy brothers had been carrying on this type of light-hearted banter over the course of several years. Bob Healy eventually sent Ed a letter challenging him to come to the IFT and prove his boast or to shut up about being the best Frisbee player in the world![2]

Well, 1968 was the year that Ed decided to actually attend the IFT and make good on his challenge, but he was a little worried since he had only five guys for his team and no back-up players. So he asked Stancil Johnson to become the sixth member of the team.

Stancil had been hoping to find a team on which to play, so he readily accepted the offer. The team consisted of Ed Headrick, his sons Dan and Gary, Jay Shelton, Steve Sewell, and now Stancil. They called themselves the California Masters, and were actually a very powerful team. Steve Sewell and Jay Shelton were two of the strongest Frisbee throwers around during that era. With the addition of Stancil Johnson to the team, they unknowingly were inheriting a secret weapon: Stancil's sidearm throw. Until the 1968 IFT, none of the Guts players had ever seen or used the sidearm throw. While it was new to them, Stancil had developed the sidearm throw early in his Frisbee throwing, and was a bit surprised that none of these Guts Frisbee players at the IFT were aware of that type of throw.[3]

---

2. See a copy of this letter to Ed Headrick from Bob Healy, Appendix J.

3. All of the Stancil Johnson information came from a long telephone interview with him in the latter part of 2011, and subsequently two audio tapes of his memoirs that he graciously sent. Thank you Stancil!

Stancil's sidearm took them by surprise and proved to be very effective. At one point Ed told Stancil not to use the sidearm too much because the veteran IFT players were getting miffed, and he was afraid the Healy brothers might try to make a rule to outlaw the throw! It turns out that with Stancil's sidearm, along with the power of Steve Sewell and Jay Shelton, the upstart California Masters team became only the second team in the eleven-year history of the IFT to defeat the Healy brothers' North Central team.

Stancil's already strong enthusiasm for Frisbee was further reinforced by meeting Ed Headrick and by his experiences at the 1968 IFT—so much so that he decided that he would write a book about Frisbee. And so he did. Seven years later the Frisbee community got its first major book about their beloved sport. It was entitled *Frisbee,* and subtitled, *A Practitioner's Manual and Definitive Treatise.* Definitive it surely was! Anything anyone wanted to know about Frisbee was in Stancil's book. Stancil introduced his book at the 1975 IFT, and it promptly fueled the big boom in disc sports that was occurring at that time. The Stancil Johnson story once again demonstrates the critically important ramifications of the IFA and its newsletter.

There are far too many other examples of how the *IFA Newsletter* was a critical catalyst to the development of disc sports to cover in our book, but they all demonstrate how important the *IFA Newsletter* was to the growth and development of a cohesive Frisbee culture. The IFA helped lay the foundation for the origin and development of all disc sports, including Disc Golf and its governing body, the Professional Disc Golf Association (PDGA).

CHAPTER 5

A CHAIN OF EVENTS

The Emergence of Disc Golf

WHAT WE HAVE SEEN SO FAR in this book is that from the very beginnings of the human species, some sort of disc-flinging activity spontaneously occurred whenever and wherever one or more of us began to interact with small hand held disc-shaped objects that had relatively good Frisbee-like aerodynamics.

It is important to understand that before the mid-1700s there were very few aerodynamic disc-shaped objects in existence. It wasn't until well into the 1700s that technological advances made the existence of tin container lids available in large enough numbers for people to produce any significant disc flinging occurrences.

But when such container lids did start appearing ubiquitously, small clusters of local disc-flinging games and activities started to appear right along with them.

Among the disc flinging games that did spontaneously appear here and there, a few of them were golf-like in nature. The game of golf preceded the appearance of tin lids by over 300 years!

By the late 1700s, the game of golf had been around long enough for a modest proportion of the population in this country (especially those of Scottish descent) to be aware of its existence, so some of these flying disc activities may have actually have been an intentional emulation of the ball and club golf game. As other people were discovering the fun of disc flinging, some of them would create a game where they counted the number of attempts it took to fling a disc-shaped object to a designated target...and then recognized that their activity was golf-like in nature.

Think in terms of our conjectural scene of Johnny discovering the fun of tossing a cookie can lid around when his mother brought a tin of cookies to him and his friends as they played outside. What if his father played golf at the local links? As Johnny and his friends escalated their new discovery of tin lid-flinging fun and started challenging each other to skill games, Johnny very well could have realized he could play golf with the lids, and they started to have a whale of a time emulating his father's game.

Never mind the fact that our Johnny is merely a conjectural account. We have firsthand historical evidence of this very thing happening in the real world, and not only before the plastic flying disc era, but repeated many times after the Frisbee and other flying discs came into being.

A perfect example and one of the earliest instances that anyone knows of golf being played with a flying disc concerns a young grade-school-age boy named Ronald Gibson, from Bladworth, Saskatchewan, Canada...a tiny burg with a total population of 115![1] In 1995, then 79-year-old Ronald Gibson was living near

1. Malafronte, *The Complete Book of Frisbee*, pages 41–42.

San Carlos, California, and happened to be reading a magazine in which Victor Malafronte had written an article about "Metal Frisbees." In that article, Victor talked about the book he was writing and asked the readers to contribute any information they had about early Frisbee Golf play.

Gibson sent a two-page letter to Victor chronicling an account of how he and a group of his Bladworth Elementary School chums discovered that they could play the game of golf with the tin lids from lard and grease containers. They laid out a course around their school grounds, and called their game "Tin Lid Golf." They drew four to five-foot diameter circles into sandy patches around the school grounds, and kept score by counting how many throws it took to land their tin lids into each of the target circles.

It seems apparent that either Gibson or one of his friends had some sort of working knowledge of the game of golf, despite living in such a small, remote Canadian village. Ron Gibson and his friends played their game of Tin Lid Golf on a fairly regular basis for a number of years, right up until their high school days, at which point they started to go their separate ways and got involved in more traditional sports and activities.

Victor Malafronte's aforementioned book includes other quite similar accounts of early Disc Golf play in the 1930s, '40s, and '50s. Some of these instances were quite involved and organized.

Former Harvard student George Snow had similarly found out about Victor Malafronte's research project and exchanged a series of three letters with him about "Can Cover Golf" and other "can cover" activities as he called them.[2] In this series of letters to Victor, Snow recounts a story that was remarkably similar to the conjectural account of Johnny and his mother's cookie can lid!

Snow tells this story, quoted directly from his December 1994 letter to Victor:

> In December 1938 I was staying with some classmates at the unofficial Harvard ski cabin on Pinkham Notch Road in New Hampshire's White Mountains. Sitting around a long table at breakfast, we got fooling around and I picked up the cover from a round tin of crackers and threw it at the guy at the other end of the table. We were all startled by its smooth level flight—I had by chance held it edge down and had given it a good back hand wrist-snap spin. For the next 10 or 15 minutes we threw the cover back and forth in the cabin—we then moved outside to a clearing and threw the cover for an hour or so, eventually moving down to the asphalt road where we soon learned to throw curves, drops, and ricochets off the pavement.

George Snow's account not only parallels the fictional Johnny, but it remarkably parallels Fred Morrison's 1937 after-Thanksgiving-dinner incident! I wasn't just kidding or guessing when I wrote that whenever people intersect with flying disc-type artifacts, eventually some of them will pick one up and fling it!

Snow further related in his letter how, when he and his friends returned to Harvard after the ski trip, they continued to enjoy the activity that they dubbed "Can Cover."

---

2. Malafronte, *The Complete Book of Frisbee*, pages 44–45

He told Victor that quite a few fellow students began to copy their can cover activities on campus. He related that the earliest he remembers playing a golf-like game with the can covers was 1939 while back home in Winchester, Massachusetts. He told of bringing the Can Cover Golf game back to the Harvard campus during the post-war '40s and playing a pick-up version of Can Cover Golf by having each competitor in turn pick out a tree, pole, or similar type of object and keeping track of how many throws it took to hit the goal. Sound familiar to anyone? Even after George Snow left Harvard, the Can Cover Golf activity still could occasionally be seen on the Harvard campus during the early 1950s.

Now, in basic infomercial jargon: "But wait! There's more!"

Eleven-year-old Tex Robertson from Sweetwater, Texas is another prime example of a person intersecting with hand-held disc-shaped objects.[3] Back in 1922, Tex and his friends discovered that tossing and catching the round metal covers from cans of shortening was a lot of fun, and it became one of their favorite activities. Tex developed a number of different disc flying activities during his subsequent years of tossing metal can covers. In the 1930s he introduced his activities to the Wolverine Day Camp in Ann Arbor, Michigan, and began to utilize the cardboard lids from the big five-gallon ice cream containers for the camp disc-flinging play.[4] Tex modified the ice cream container lids by using tape to reinforce the rims, and gluing a circular piece of felt to the top of the container to enhance their durability and flight characteristics.

---

3. Malafronte, *The Complete Book of Frisbee*, pages 39–41
4. I've tried ice cream container lids and they fly very well indeed! —*Jim*

Tex would instruct the kids at the day camp to sail the cardboard containers low and level for best results. Both the name they gave their handmade flying discs and the name they gave the disc activities that they invented eventually became known as "Sa-Lo."

In 1939, Tex moved to Burritt, Texas, where he and his wife started up a summer camp and called it Camp Long Horn. Sa-Lo activities became an integral part of Camp Long Horn. One of those activities was throwing for accuracy to a hoop-like target which soon led Tex to coming up with "Sa-Lo Golf." He laid out a five-hole course and "Sa-Lo Golf" became a regular camp activity.

Yet another example of early pre-plastic Disc Golf was the earlier-mentioned Walter Darby of Great Neck, New York who applied and won a patent in 1937 for his "Disc Scaling Game"—a Disc Golf-like game complete with basket "holes" in which to "hole out."[5]

While the known number of instances of playing golf with pre-plastic flying discs is relatively small, they significantly illustrate the point that Disc Golf-like games spontaneously emerged whenever people played with flying discs on a regular basis. None of these and other similar instances were linked to one another. These examples of early Disc Golf were discovered on their own. They each had their own isolated little core of Disc Golf play which didn't spread. None of them have any historical continuity with today's sport of Disc Golf, and none of them had any influence upon the origin of the organized sport of Disc Golf. Tex Robertson's Camp Longhorn is unique within

5. Malafronte, *The Complete Book of Frisbee*, pages 42–43

this group in that its Sa-Lo Golf activity didn't fade away as did all the rest of the known occurrences. Camp Longhorn stayed the course and grew into the largest and most successful summer camp for kids in the state of Texas...and is still going strong today! When the Morrison, Robes, and Wham-O plastic flying disc era came into being, Camp Longhorn adopted the new plastic discs as they became available, which enhanced and encouraged the continuance of its Sa-Lo Golf activity.

No one knew about Camp Longhorn or the other early instances of Disc Golf until Victor Malafronte's fabulous research uncovered the information about them. In each instance, except for Camp Longhorn, the concept of Disc Golf faded out of existence, only to wait for the next individual or group somewhere else to discover it all over again. Another commonality was that in each case, the people associated with this early Disc Golf play didn't know of any other instances of Disc Golf play, or for that matter, any other disc play period. For all they knew, they were unique in their discovery and were content to enjoy their play without any fanfare.

After plastic flying discs were produced in 1948, the number of instances of localized Disc Golf began to escalate. Each discovery included a subsequent period of playing the game with varying degrees of regularity. Some evolved into semi-organized play with small contests and competitions.

As Wham-O's Pluto Platter and Bill Robes's Space Saucer began to make a mark for themselves in the mid-1950s the plastic flying disc was still a novel item that attracted media attention. Entrepreneurs tend to notice trends like that and try to get in on the action before it is too late. Two companies from the

New York City area both started to make and market copycat plastic flying discs: the "Mars Platter" from Premier Products, and the "Zo-Lar" from Empire Plastics.

A third company, the Copar Plastic Company in Chicago, also got in on the action, making a disc called the "Sky Saucer." Around 1960 they packaged and sold their Sky Saucers in a game called "Sky Croquet." This game included a set of six Sky Saucer discs, six wire ring targets, and a detailed set of rules for playing Sky Croquet. Apparently they either had thought up the

SOME WAYS TO HAVE FUN WITH YOUR 'SKY SAUCERS'

1.	'SKY SAUCER' CATCH	-- Sail SKY SAUCER to another person .. catch, and sail it back.
2.	'SKY SAUCER'GOLF	-- Mark 9 paper picnic plates (or 9 pieces of round cardboard) with numbers 1 through 9. Place on ground in pattern to make your own 9 hole miniature golf course. Stand about 25 feet from No. 1 Hole (cardboard) and sail SKY SAUCER at the Hole. Stand next to No. 1 Hole when playing for No. 2 Hole, etc. Saucer must be touching hole to hole out. Establish pars according to distance between holes, and hazards or traps involved. Score like golf, low score wins.
3.	'SKY SAUCER'HORSESHOES	-- Put 2 pegs or sticks in the ground 15 to 20 feet apart... Let them stick up about 6 inches... Standing beside 1 peg sail SKY SAUCERS at the other... Closest, 1 point... Leaner, 2 points... Game, 11 points.
4.	'SKY SAUCER' BASKETS	-- Place empty waste basket, carton or other container from 10 to 15 feet away and sail SKY SAUCERS into basket.... Score 1 for each basket... Game 5 points... Fun indoors, too.

© COPAR 1962

concept of Disc Golf on their own, or had noticed some of the burgeoning discoveries of Disc Golf play at that time, because the fourth page of the rule book for their Sky Croquet game was entitled: "Play Sky Golf too!"[6] The Sky Golf rules were as well written as any in-a-nutshell description of Disc Golf that anyone could write about today's version of the game.

But for whatever reason, the marketing effort for Sky Croquet was unsuccessful and the game disappeared from the scene soon after its introduction. Sky Golf was gone before anyone took notice. It had no influence whatsoever upon the development of today's game. It was long after Disc Golf had already become a full-blown sport before an old Sky Croquet game was discovered by a disc collector. If it weren't for the legions of modern day flying disc collectors trying to hunt down every disc ever made, the few Copar discs still in existence might have remained hidden, and the Sky Croquet game with its Sky Golf description very well might have faded into oblivion, undiscovered and unnoticed.

There are many, many other instances of Disc Golf being independently discovered in the early plastic era. For emphasis, we will described a few of them, but please understand that they represent only the tip of the iceberg of early Disc Golf play. We will list these case histories somewhat chronologically after Fred Morrison's original Pipco Flyin-Saucer first hit the market.

Case History 1—Dan "Stork" Roddick and his father "Papa" Jack were very enthusiastic disc flingers from the early plastic flying disc era and enjoyed a variety of different ways to have fun with a flying disc. They played a golf-like flying saucer game in which

6 See Appendix I.

they would count the number of throws it would take for each of them to get their Flyin Saucer to a series of "Mother Ships," metallic rings that Jack had placed around each of the trees in his spacious Shippensburg, Pennsylvania yard. It is interesting to note that Jack says that he was fully aware that the game was a form of golf, but Dan says that it didn't occur to him that their rudimentary game was connected to golf until much later in his disc flying years. He was only five years old at the time, so we will cut him a break this time.

Case History 2—In 1957, a ten-year-old imaginative and creative kid named Phil Kennedy had a keen interest in rockets, experimental airplanes, and the UFO-flying saucer phenomenon that were all popular topics in the mid-fifties press. One early spring day, while shopping at his local five-and-dime store in Wethersfield, Connecticut, his eye caught sight of something new and interesting—a floor display bin full of Pluto Platters looking for all the world like miniature flying saucers, with portholes on the cockpit, and the names of the planets engraved around the rim. With his imagination soaring, it was a sure sale for the store! Young Phil plunked down his full week's allowance and walked out with his treasure. He soon got the hang of making it fly, and enlisted his older brother Rick to join him in order to cut down on the retrieval time between throws.

In subsequent days and weeks he showed his friends his new Pluto Platter Flying Saucer and engaged them in tossing and catching it. Phil did not overlook the Pluto Platter's iconic backside engraving: "To Fly, Flip Away Backhanded. Flat Flip Flies Straight, Tilted Flip Curves. EXPERIMENT!" and its accompanying second line "Play Catch—Invent Games."

He experimented and invented games. One day when he was left without anyone to toss with, he challenged himself to see how few throws it would take to hit the telephone pole across from his house. His father was an avid ball golfer, and it was not long before Phil realized he, too, was playing golf. He subsequently enjoined his neighborhood friends to play the game with him, and it became one of their regular activities. Since it was the spring of 1957, Wham-O had not yet discovered the name "Frisbee," let alone added it to their line of discs, so Phil called his new game "Pluto Platter Golf."

Above: Hole one of Phil Kennedy's Pluto Platter Golf course laid out in the spring of 1957. That telephone pole across the street is the target.

Right: The actual first style Wham-O Pluto Platter Phil used to play Pluto Platter Golf in 1957.

As Phil succumbed to the inevitable "getting-older" syndrome, his Disc Golf activities took a back seat to more traditional school sports and interests (with girls mixed in, of course). But he did bring his Pluto Platter with him to college, and passed along the concept of Disc Golf to dorm friends and fraternity brothers. Phil engaged in enough Frisbee activity now and then so as not to forget about it altogether. The Pluto Platter tagged along with Phil post-college, after marriage, and during a stint in the Navy, idling in the background until 1976 when Phil intersected with the serious interest in disc sports being driven by the IFA and its North American Series (NAS) tournaments. He got caught up in Frisbee and Disc Golf all over again... this time for keeps.

Phil was a 1950s version of Ronald Gibson, showing his friends his Disc Golf game and playing it with them on a regular basis. The difference between Phil and Ronald Gibson was that Phil maintained his connection with Frisbee and his Disc Golf game long enough to eventually encounter the IFA and the NAS tournaments that came along. He joined in on many of the events and became part of the evolution of disc sports. The book that Phil co-authored with Fred Morrison, *Flat Flip Files Straight,* is an exceptionally accurate and exquisitely interesting account of the origin and history of *the* Frisbee disc. It is also a beautifully done tome on disc collecting. Fred and Phil's book is a highly recommended read for anyone who wants the true story of where the Frisbee brand disc came from, and how Wham-O got involved with disc marketing. And it is a disc collector's must. Furthermore, it was Phil's expertise and graphic arts abilities that were responsible for getting this particular book about the origin of Disc Golf published and out to you.

Case History 3—In the very same time period as Phil's, nine-year-old creative and imaginative Bob "Flash" Kingsley also bought a Pluto Platter. Flash proceeded to interact with his Pluto Platter in a very similar manner in his backyard in Fayetteville, New York. Flash, like Phil, just wasn't the type to stop tossing his Pluto Platter around merely because he couldn't find a companion with whom to share his activity, so he, too, quickly discovered that he could play golf with his Pluto Platter. Not only that, he was intrigued by trying to see how long he could make it fly before he caught his own throw. He actually beat BFG guru Roger Barrett to the punch and discovered MTA many years before Roger introduced it to the BFG members!

Flash's family moved to Massachusetts in 1958, and little did he know that he was living almost within Frisbee-tossing distance to future Frisbee stars Tom McCrann and Dave Johnson...only to meet up with them 16 years later when the *IFA Newsletter* eventually brought the three of them together in their common quest for Frisbee play. Right through high school, college, and his Army days, Flash continued his flying disc activities, and collared anybody who was willing (or polite enough) to hear all about Disc Golf, MTA, and Frisbee tossing in general. During a stint in the Army, Flash laid out several Disc Golf courses in North Carolina, and further spread the idea of Disc Golf to his acquaintances. Spurred on by the *IFA Newsletter*, Flash ultimately traveled to the IFT in 1973, where he met the mainstream of the Frisbee community for the first time, including Dan "Stork" Roddick—forging a partnership that turned out to be an overwhelmingly significant key to the development of disc sports, which will be discussed further along in the book.

Case History 4—We certainly don't want to forget Lightnin' Lyle Jensen, one of the more creative and colorful modern-era Frisbee practitioners that the *IFA Newsletter* attracted to the mix. Lyle also started with a Pluto Platter in 1957, throwing it around with his brother and his father. Somewhere between the time his father brought home the Pluto Platter and the summer of 1958, Lyle and his brother Craig developed a Disc Golf game around the Jensen home and holed-out by hitting trees, a fire hydrant, and the two steel clothesline poles Lightnin's father had cemented in the backyard. From that point on, right up through college, Lightnin' enjoyed playing and inventing Frisbee games. In fact, while attending St. Cloud State College in central Minnesota, he and a college pal came up with a game very much like today's Double Disc Court, only they called it "Dilemma."

Lyle was an important member of a group of avid Frisbee players in the Twin Cities area who were instrumental in starting up the Minnesota Frisbee Association in 1975. Lyle went on to design several Disc Golf courses in Minnesota, and helped to lay the groundwork for Minneapolis to host one of the big NAS tournaments of 1976. Lightnin' Lyle is also one of the world's foremost experts on collecting the Pluto Platter. He's even incorporated his love of flying disc activities with his life-long passion for cartooning.

Case History 5—Yet another instance of late-fifties/early-sixties Disc Golf discovery is exemplified by the Kevin Donnelly Story. Similar to all of the previous accounts, Kevin bought a Frisbee in 1959 and became enthused with its possibilities. He, too, put together a Disc Golf-like game and called it "Street Frisbee Golf." Kevin and his Costa Mesa, California neighborhood friends would keep track of how many throws it would take to get the Frisbee around the block. In 1961, while working as a recreation leader for the Newport Beach Parks and Recreation Department, Kevin set up a 6-hole Disc Golf course, designating specific trees and light poles to hit as the targets. His Frisbee Golf program was popular with the kids and Kevin expanded it to a weekly activity. In 1962, due to the popularity of his program, he was asked to set up similar Frisbee Golf courses in two more of the Newport Beach Parks and Recreation facilities.

Kevin eventually obtained his B.S. in Recreation Management from Los Angeles State College and went on to obtain his M.S. degree from San Francisco State College in May of 1965. Upon graduation, the city of Newport Beach hired him as the Recreation Supervisor for the Parks, Beaches, and Recreation Department. He managed a staff of twenty recreation leaders and was in charge of recreational activities for nine city parks. He taught the recreation leaders the Frisbee Golf game and encouraged them to incorporate it into their weekly activity schedules at all nine parks.

In October 1965, Kevin organized a big Newport Beach Recreation Department Frisbee Golf tournament. He drove to San Gabriel, California to visit the headquarters of Wham-O, seeking their help in sponsoring the event. Wham-O donated Frisbee discs, Super Balls, Hula Hoops, and Air Blasters for the occasion.

Because of the dearth of trees at the site selected for the tournament, Kevin came up with the idea of using Hula Hoops attached vertically to two wooden stakes as the targets for the event—an idea that was eventually reused by Wham-O four years later at the November 1969 All Comers Meet.[7]

Case History 6—Previously we wrote about George Sappenfield discovering Disc Golf while a college student at Fresno State in 1965 and how after college he hooked up with Wham-O as a Frisbee promotions consultant. Later in the book we will talk more about the critically important role that George played in Disc Golf becoming the world-wide sport that we know of today. For now, it is enough to understand that George also perfectly illustrates the concept of how, before the *IFA Newsletter* was created, people enthused with Frisbee Golf play had no way of knowing about others beyond their local area who were also enthusiastically involved with flying disc activity. It turns out that at the same time, and in the same California area, George Sappenfield was playing and promoting Disc Golf in almost the same manner as Kevin Donnelly, but totally independent of Donnelly's activities. Quite serendipitously, their paths crossed a year later in 1966 when George, as a college student in a recreation major program, had Kevin Donnelly as his professor for a recreation course at Fresno State College! Because of their mutual interest in Frisbee Golf activities, they became friends outside of the classroom. Their parallel activity promoting Disc Golf represents one of the largest and most organized of the early examples of Disc Golf discovery.

7. Information about Kevin Donnelly came from an article that Don Altmyer wrote and submitted to the PDGA for their archives.

Case History 7—Similar to Kevin Donnelly and George Sappenfield's Disc Golf activities in California recreation programs, but again totally independent from them, was a mid-1960s parks and recreation program in Michigan that set up a Frisbee Golf course and put on a tournament for the kids virtually in the exact same manner that both Kevin Donnelly and George Sappenfield did in California. (Unfortunately, due to a computer glitch, I lost the PDF of the 1965 newspaper article that described this event so I can't be more specific on the details, or reference the source properly. The PDF copy of the news article was sent to me by Martin Hain, one the most thorough Frisbee researchers of all time. He is in the same league as Victor Malafronte and Phil Kennedy; in other words, at the very top of the mountain! This book would not have been possible without the help of those three guys.)

Case History 8—Another example of independent Disc Golf discovery in the early sixties is previously mentioned Jay Shelton, who discovered the concept of playing golf with a Frisbee much in the same way that Phil Kennedy, Flash Kingsley, and Kevin Donnelly did back in 1950s. He kept at Frisbee flinging and Frisbee Golf play during his Harvard days, and then, when he went on to graduate school at the University of California at Berkeley in 1968, he met up with the group of Frisbee enthusiasts that became known as the BFG. It was Jay who introduced the concept of Frisbee Golf to the BFG, and who helped design the Berkeley campus object course that was a regular part of the BFG's activities.

Case History 9—The Southern California Olsen family—Jim and his sons Jim and Joe—were dabbling with Disc Golf totally independently during the 1960s. The Olsens are a great example of early independent discoverers of Disc Golf who continued their personal and obscure Disc Golf play right up until the time that the organized sport of Disc Golf emerged. They enthusiastically got involved with the sport and have continued to play the game ever since.

Case History 10—The campus of the University of California, Santa Cruz was the scene of another example. About 1968, a small group of guys were playing Frisbee around the campus on a fairly regular basis. Steve Weldon and his friend Pierre Zetterberg came up with a game they called "Travel Frisbee." While playing their game one day, Steve turned to Pierre and asked him, "Why can't we play golf with this thing?"[8] Well, they soon *did* start to play golf with their Frisbee discs. They laid out a 13-hole course on the campus, and showed other students their Frisbee Golf game. It eventually resulted in an intramural Frisbee Golf tournament being held on campus in May of 1970.

Case History 11—Jack Barry met Doug McCrae at Goose Rocks Beach in Kennebunkport, Maine in 1964. Due to their mutual interest in Frisbee flinging, they often played Frisbee together during the summer seasons. Jack reports that both he and Doug were from golfing families, and they eventually realized they could play golf with their Frisbee discs. By 1968 they were playing eighteen holes of Frisbee Golf as they traversed up the street, designating telephone poles, mailboxes, and large boulders to hit along the way. They also laid out an eighteen-hole course on the beach, drawing circles in the sand for the holes and rectangles for the tee boxes.[9]

---

8. This is a direct quote from an email message Steve Weldon sent to Kevin "Skippy Jammer" Givens, Frisbee player extraordinaire, on October 9, 2009.

9. This info is from Jack Barry, sent in an email message dated March 9, 2012.

Case History 12—Ed Babb and his brother Bobby from Portland, Maine also discovered a form of Frisbee Golf on their own in the late sixties. Every now and then during their Frisbee tossing and catching, they would randomly pick out an object to hit in a designated number of throws. By 1971, it had occurred to Ed that that type of activity was really like playing golf and that they could string out a series of the selected objects mimicking a golf course.[10] When Ed discovered the NAS tournaments in 1976, he got hooked into Frisbee big time, and joined the PDGA as member number 213. He went on to become a significant competitor and an important promoter of Disc Golf in the Northeastern part of the country.

Case History 13—John Schaberg of Devon, Pennsylvania had a little help along the way from the little raccoon that was his constant companion everywhere he went. I have no doubt in my mind that there are some people playing Disc Golf today because of being attracted to that cute little raccoon rather than being intrigued by the CPI All Star discs that John was using at that time.

The escalating discovery of Disc Golf beginning in the mid-1960s was partly due to the traditional game of ball golf becoming better known and immensely more popular among the general public. As television began featuring the exciting play of Arnold Palmer, Jack Nicklaus, and many others, the already well-established game of golf was thrust into the national limelight and grabbed the attention of many golfers and non-golfers alike. Prior to this TV popularization of golf, many non-golfers had known the game existed, but felt that

10. This info came in a series of email exchanges with Ed Babb prior to March 2012.

golf was an elite activity for the wealthy, and was not for them. So even if they happened to have heard about someone playing golf with flying discs, it didn't register. But when television started covering golf in a major way, there was an ever-increasing number of people tuned in to the favorable attributes of golf, and correspondingly, more people began to discover that golf could be played with Frisbees.

Now that we have laid the groundwork, we can finally get to the story of the origin of the organized sport of competitive Disc Golf! Unlike with the discoveries of Disc Golf activity in general, we can trace the origin of the organized sport of Disc Golf and its PDGA governing body to a specific set of circumstances. These all happened within a short period of time and enabled the growing number of independent local epicenters of Disc Golf to come together and to evolve into the organized competitive sport.

We will start with some questions. If people were discovering Disc Golf from very early on, why didn't the organized sport of Disc Golf emerge much earlier than 1974? What happened in 1974 that didn't happen before then?

The answer to these questions starts with the principle of "Disc Golf Critical Density." This principle is based upon the premise that until there is a high enough percentage of people playing Disc Golf on a regular basis, interest in Disc Golf within any local pocket of Disc Golf play could not easily be spread to others beyond the local area.

Ronald Gibson and his grade school friends of 1926 are a perfect example of the "Disc Golf Critical Density" principle. They discovered that they could play golf with tin lids and had fun with the game for a number of years. But how many other people in their immediate geographical area were avid tin-lid golfers? Maybe zero? I'd conjecture that most of the people who knew Ronald Gibson and his friends thought these youngsters were quite creative in the way that they emulated the "grownup" game of ball golf, but didn't give much thought to trying it themselves. When these kids got older, finished high school, and went their separate ways, there was nobody left behind to pick up the mantle of "Tin Lid Golf," and spread the interest to new people. Their game naturally faded into obscurity. There just weren't enough tin-lid flingers to sustain the game. Had there been a higher number of people in that geographical area playing games with tin lids, maybe the "Tin Lid Golf" game might have been passed on to newcomers and spread out to others. It may have continued to grow even after the originators of the game moved on to other stages of life. But that did not happen.

This same sort of thing occurred with all the Disc Golf play in the thirties, forties, fifties, and even into the sixties as the plastic era of disc flying caught on. There still wasn't a high enough density of disc enthusiasts to propagate the game of Disc Golf. That is why the Copar Sky Golf game of 1960 never caught on. Even after Wham-O started marketing the Frisbee and its popularity grew in the mid-sixties, the isolated pockets of Disc Golf that developed here and there increased in number, but gained no real momentum toward becoming a unified competitive sport.

Although Kevin Donnelly and George Sappenfield were actively promoting Disc Golf play and competition in California throughout the later 1960s, the game still didn't catch on as a sport. This was despite Kevin Donnelly including the concept of Disc Golf in the curriculum of the recreation course he was teaching at Fresno State College in 1966, and George Sappenfield actually getting hired by Wham-O as a consultant to promote Frisbee Disc play. George did succeed in convincing Wham-O to set up a nine-hole Disc Golf course for the All Comers Meet as previously described. But for some reason Wham-O just didn't feel that the Disc Golf game would fit into their marketing strategy, and declined to go forward with it after that November 1969 meet.

The prevailing theory explaining Wham-O's lack of interest in Disc Golf is two-fold. One, they didn't perceive that Disc Golf was a high-priority activity among the Frisbee enthusiasts with whom they were involved at that time—specifically, the IFT-centered Guts community.

And two, Wham-O's primary marketing theme for their Frisbees was simplicity. "Easy-to-use-and-understand" was a key theme for the promotion of all their products. Frisbee Golf, with its relatively elaborate creation of tee areas and setting up the vertical Hula Hoops for the "holes," didn't quite satisfy that test for simplicity.

The Guts game that Wham-O was promoting at that time had the element of simplicity they were looking for, and they felt it had the most potential for promoting the fun of simple toss-and-catch games. They even came up with a special disc for the game of Guts, the original Fastback Frisbee model, and included a description for Guts in each package in hopes of enticing more people to play Guts.

Frisbee Golf became virtually nonexistent in Wham-O's eyes as they forged ahead with promoting the annual IFT. They put

George Sappenfield in charge of developing and promoting the National Junior Frisbee Championship program for the younger kids, but they specifically constrained him from including Disc Golf as part of the Junior Program.

Another clear example of this Wham-O thinking was Goldy Norton's *The Official Frisbee Handbook*. Goldy wrote and published that little book for Wham-O in 1972. It was the end-all be-all source of information about Frisbee at that time. It talked about the origins and lore of Frisbee, and describes in detail every known game or activity being played with a Frisbee at that time...except for Frisbee or Disc Golf. That topic is absent from the book. It really is a great little book—as complete a tome on Frisbee as you could find in 1972. Except for a description of Disc Golf, it had it all. The book was an overall reflection on what Wham-O had in mind for the marketing of their Frisbee disc. The first pages describe the lore and origins of Frisbee; the next twenty-five pages show photos of early Frisbee icons Spyder Wills and Victor Malafronte demonstrating all the throws and catches that could be done with a Frisbee. Plain and simple fun.

The book then follows up with twenty-one pages of games and activities that can be played with a Frisbee. The section begins with a paragraph or two describing activities such as "Sweet Georgia Brown," "Follow the Leader," "Keep Away," "By the Book," "Hit the Spot," and seven other similarly obscure, but simple activities.

Included at the end of this section of the book are several pages of text and photographs of Guts, the very game that was responsible for Wham-O's decision to keep the Frisbee in their product line. There are also another couple of pages devoted to the new game on the scene: Ultimate. But nothing about the nature of Disc Golf! This was despite the fact that Wham-O consultant George Sappenfield kept urging them to promote Frisbee Golf, always referring to the success that the activity had at the All Comers Meet. But to no avail.

The lack of promotion of Frisbee Golf by Wham-O and the lack of critical density worked together to delay the advent of the organized sport of Disc Golf.

Thus, before 1974, Disc Golf did not exist as an organized sport. In 1973, except for Guts Frisbee and the rapidly growing new sport of Ultimate, no organized disc sports of *any* other kind existed. But the year 1973 was when "Disc Golf Critical Density" was reached.

CHAPTER 6

A CHAIN OF EVENTS

1974: The Organized Sport of Disc Golf is Born

NOW WE ARE READY for the details of the origin of the sport of Disc Golf. The "Big Bang" of Disc Golf so to speak. Flash Kingsley met Dan Roddick at the 1973 IFT, and together they forged a partnership that led to previously unheard of disc sport organization. The core of the rapidly burgeoning Ultimate Frisbee community attended the 1973 IFT, and learned of Frisbee Golf and other nascent disc sports. They brought Frisbee Golf info back to their Ultimate teammates. The Guts community also learned of Frisbee Golf and a variety of other disc activities to complement their Guts game. Critical density arrived at the 1973 IFT. The fuse was ready; the only thing needed at this point was a spark to ignite the fuse. Something had to happen that would catch the attention of the *IFA Newsletter* and the news media in general.

In 1974 several critical events provided the spark that set off the Big Bang of Disc Golf.

The first part of the story actually begins in 1970 with one of the spontaneous discoveries of Disc Golf, similar in many ways to all the other scenarios that took place from the very beginning of disc play. Only this time, the enthusiasm with Frisbee Golf and other disc play peaked precisely at the point when Disc Golf's critical density had been reached. There is something to be said for serendipity!

This particular incidence of Disc Golf discovery involved two brothers at Green Lakes State Park near Syracuse, New York. Let me state up front that one of the authors of this book, I, Jim Palmeri, was the older of the two brothers. So this section of the book is autobiographical in nature.

In 1970, I wasn't a Frisbee player yet, and had no concept or knowledge of any Frisbee activities, either locally or anywhere else. My first encounter with a Frisbee occurred on Mother's Day 1970, when all my siblings gathered at our parents' house to celebrate the occasion. I am a competitive fellow who enjoys all sorts of sports and games, and figured that I would organize a two-on-two touch football game with my brother John and our two brothers-in-law. I presented my idea to the three guys and they concurred that it would be fun. I grabbed my football and went out to the yard to set up the boundaries for the game and then I waited. In the next five minutes, no one showed up. As I was just about to run back into the house to find out what the holdup was, my brother came out and said that the other two would be coming soon. He brought two Frisbee discs with him: a green Regular Model, and a purple Pro Model with a single gold band hot stamp. He suggested we toss them around while waiting for our brothers-in-law to get off their duffs and show up.

I scoffed and told him to put those silly things down and to toss the football back and forth with me. He reluctantly agreed, for a few minutes at least, and then complained about how boring that was, and that it would be way more fun to fling a Frisbee back and forth. I reluctantly agreed to give it a try. I didn't do very well, because I had never thrown a Frisbee before. But it was kind of fun, and after a few minutes of toss and catch, the creative side of me took over and I suggested that we try to toss both discs back and forth simultaneously. That was even more fun! Then the competitive side of me kicked in and I suggested that we make a game out of the double disc activity. I told my brother that we should try to time our throws so as to force one another to touch both Frisbees at the same time. We decided that each time one of us succeeded in forcing the other to do so, he would be awarded a point. The first one to reach eleven points would be the winner. The birth of Double Disc Court! We had so much fun that we didn't even notice that our brothers-in-law hadn't come out to play touch football yet, and when we finally did notice, we didn't care; our new game was too much fun to stop for plain old touch football!

We called our new game "Court Frisbee." (Its name didn't get shortened to DDC until four years later.) We played our new game on a fairly regular basis from that point on, and it led to my becoming quite enthused with Frisbee activity in general.

Two months later, in August of 1970, my brother and I spent the weekend camping in Green Lakes State Park, near Syracuse, New York. While walking back to our campsite after a session of Court Frisbee, I pointed out a particular tree down the pathway about 65 to 75 yards from us. I challenged my bother to a contest to see who could fling their disc to the tree in fewer throws. He asked me how we should determine that we were "to the tree." I pondered for a moment and told him that when you land your Frisbee within one disc diameter from the base of the tree you are "at" the tree. I am not sure why we didn't consider hitting the tree to determine the outcome, but we didn't. It just seemed that having the disc come to rest within one disc width from the base of the tree was as good a way as any to determine when we got our disc to the tree. It took us both three throws. We agreed on another tree to break the tie. The distance to the second tree was slightly farther than to the first one, but we both succeeded in three throws again. I said "Okay, let's try again…but this time we will make it tougher." I scanned the area for a good target and saw a playground that seemed the proper distance away. In this playground was a small children's sand box, about six feet square. I suggested that the winner of our contest would be whoever could land their disc in the sandbox in fewer throws. But I told my brother that we had to make it challenging to make sure we broke the tie. I pointed out a tree about half way to the sandbox and to the left a bit, and said that we must first go around that tree to the left, like a dog leg in golf…. Then it hit me! I exclaimed to my brother, "Hey John, do you know what we're doing? *We're playing golf!"*

I was ecstatic to discover that I could play one of my favorite sports—golf—quite inexpensively relative to the steep cost of the standard ball and club game. The costs involved and the unavailability of golf courses meant that I played ball golf much too infrequently to satisfy my desire for the game. But when I discovered that I could play the game of golf with my Frisbees, I no longer lamented that I couldn't afford to play the traditional version as often as I wanted to. Now I could play golf anytime and just about anywhere.

And I did. I set out to emulate the ball golf game as closely as I could. Wherever I laid out a course, I looked for existing objects into which I could throw my disc...the "hole" so to speak. I used old tires, trash barrels, or bins of any kind that were lying around my apartment complex or the particular park I was visiting at the time. If there were not enough receptacle-type items available, I would supplement with some cardboard boxes that I kept on hand just for my Frisbee Golf play. I never thought to hit an object to simulate holing out. I was a golfer, and golfers putt the ball *into* a hole. It was just the natural thing for me. When I played ball golf, I didn't slam the ball into the flag stick, or into a tree, or a bench, or a telephone pole. I would always putt the ball into a hole. So now, playing Frisbee Golf, I always looked for a ball golf putting simulation in my attempt to emulate the game as closely as possible.

By September 1970, a month after discovering my new passion, I held my first tournament, dubbing it the "Canandaigua Open." The name came from the lake at which I had rented a cottage for a week's vacation. I set up a nine-hole course around the cottage grounds, incorporating the shoreline of the lake for some out-of-bounds risk. An old automobile tire was the target for one hole; several trash barrels served as receptacles for other holes; and an old wooden box lying near the cottage was yet another hole. I used several cardboard boxes to fill in as the receptacles for the remainder of the nine-hole course. The signature hole was a full 360-degree clockwise loop around the cottage itself, holing out to the rubber tire that also served as the tee marker. It was the lone par-five hole.

I invited a group of friends for a big overnight party at the cottage. A keg of beer, good food, and two rounds on the nine-hole course were the highlights of the party. The Canandaigua Open was a fun-filled success, and further whet my appetite for my newly discovered way of playing the game of golf. I was hooked.

The football season and winter ensued, but despite not getting to play Frisbee Golf much, I didn't forget about it. When the spring of 1971 came around, Frisbee Golf became a regular recreational activity again, along with the Court Frisbee game that I had invented. I would gather together my brother and a small group of friends for a round of Frisbee Golf and some Court Frisbee competition as often as I could. When no one showed up, I would go it alone, experimenting with different course designs. Our small group had absolutely no knowledge of the existence of the IFA, its newsletter, or any other Frisbee activity at all. The only people we knew who had ever played with a Frisbee were ourselves and any friends we managed to get to come and play Frisbee Golf and Court Frisbee with us.

But regardless of our delusion that we were the only ones in the world playing Frisbee Golf, we enjoyed it and Court Frisbee thoroughly, and capped off the 1971 summer season with a somewhat formal Frisbee championship event in conjunction with a Labor Day hot dog cookout that I hosted at my place. The event consisted of a Court Frisbee bracketed tournament and two rounds of Frisbee Golf on a nine-hole course that I had laid out around my apartment complex. Unfortunately, the records of who won are long gone and memories of many details are also pretty well wiped out. What I know for certain, though, is that I finished near the bottom in that first-ever DDC competition, proving early on that just because I invented the game didn't mean I could play it well. (That still applies to this very day!) However, I recall that I performed well in the Frisbee Golf event. There were only two guys in our group who had ever beaten me: my brother John, and my friend John Pierce. My brother didn't make it to the picnic, so most likely the worst I finished was second place.

The significant point is that the event really increased my interest in the game of Frisbee Golf. When the spring of 1972 came around, Frisbee Golf was foremost on my mind, and I created a semi-permanent eighteen-hole layout at Ontario Beach Park, the gateway to Lake Ontario in the City of Rochester, New York. The eighteen-hole layout utilized the standard park trash barrels as the targets for holing out. For the few holes that didn't have convenient trash barrel placements, I used portable cardboard boxes that I brought along each time we played the course.

As warm spring weather began to arrive, I looked for opportunities to play Frisbee more often, so I organized a Court Frisbee and Frisbee Golf league which met every Tuesday evening at my newly created Ontario Beach Park Frisbee Golf course. The layout had eighteen different tee-off locations—although several holes shared the same trash barrel goal. This was not a big inconvenience since it was essentially a private course with no more than two or three groups playing at any one time. On many of the Tuesday nights we were lucky to get five or six players to show up. No one else knew the course existed, or even about the concept of Frisbee Golf. We virtually had the course all to ourselves, and only occasionally had to wait for a few people who were strolling through the course area on the way to the beach, pier, or one of the park pavilions. It was like our private country club. There were never more than fifteen or twenty people in the park on any Tuesday evening.

At first, the small group of players attending the Tuesday night league consisted of me, my brother John, my friend John Pierce, my babysitter's boyfriend Bruce, and two of Bruce's friends, Wally "Genesee Cream Ale" Wallenhorst and Tom Fox.

In an effort to expand the size of the small group of people taking part in the league, and to find other people who enjoyed competitive Frisbee play, I posted flyers about our Frisbee club's activities on the bulletin boards of all the Rochester area colleges. This had no significant effect. Only two people responded to these posted notices all summer long. We relied on word of mouth to friends and acquaintances in an attempt to drum up more interest.

After a while interest did begin to grow—as many as eight to ten people started showing up on Tuesday evenings. I decided to hold a formal "City of Rochester Frisbee Championships" event featuring Court Frisbee and Frisbee Golf.

Word-of-mouth promotion and another round of notices posted at local college campuses and grocery stores resulted in thirteen people showing up on Saturday, August 5, 1972 at Ontario Beach Park for the City of Rochester Frisbee Championship. The tournament got excellent newspaper coverage with a large write-up in the Sunday edition of the Rochester *Democrat and Chronicle*. The event was a huge success, with perfect weather and a grand time had by all thirteen participants. The tournament introduced Frisbee play as a competitive activity first-hand to at least four or five new people. With a Sunday edition circulation of over 200,000, the newspaper article, complete with photos of the happening, indirectly introduced the concept of competitive Frisbee play to many thousands more. This resulted in a few new people showing up on subsequent Tuesday evenings for the rest of the summer.

Because of the cold winter winds at Ontario Beach Park and Rochester in general, we reluctantly took a long break from Frisbee Golf and Court Frisbee. But we were eager to restart our weekly Tuesday evening gatherings in the spring of 1973, and found that the number of participants was somewhat larger each week than the previous year...even as high as fifteen or so on some nights.

Because of the great success we had with the 1972 City of Rochester Frisbee Championships, we repeated the event again during the 1973 season. Again the weather was perfect, and this time the number of participants doubled. We had 26 competitors!

But the greatest significance of the 1973 Tournament was the fact that one participant brought a copy of the most recent *IFA Newsletter.* Remember, up until that point, neither I nor any of the other regular Rochester Frisbee Club members had ever heard of the International Frisbee Association or the *IFA Newsletter.* After three years of Frisbee play, we still thought we were a unique group enjoying the Court Frisbee game I had created, and the Frisbee Golf game that I had discovered. Outside of our Rochester Frisbee Club activities, and Tuesday night league play, none of us had ever seen or heard of anyone else playing with a Frisbee, either for competitive activities, or even merely tossing it back and forth. We truly, but naively, thought we were the only ones on the planet enthusiastic enough to spend so much time and energy organizing weekly league play and promoting annual city-wide Frisbee tournaments. I foolishly thought Frisbee Golf was nonexistent outside of Rochester! I had no way of knowing otherwise.

I was 33 years old at that time and my peers were all working people doing the standard recreational sports: softball, touch football, golf, hunting, fishing, hiking, archery, etc. Several times I was told by some of my more stodgy peers that perhaps it was time for me to put my Frisbee toys aside and get involved with the more mainstream recreational activities, particularly the traditional ball golf game I had previously played with them on occasion. I didn't accept any of that advice. But the attitude of my peers further reinforced my feelings that our Frisbee Golf and other Frisbee play were unique.

So imagine my extreme surprise when I saw that copy of the *IFA Newsletter* and read about a whole plethora of Frisbee activities, including this particular tidbit: "Frisbee Golf is being popularized in Devon, Pennslyvania, where John Schaberg and his group have set up a sixteen-hole course and an eighteen-hole course."[1]

My mouth dropped wide open and I excitedly exclaimed, "Hey look at this! We aren't the only ones playing Frisbee Golf! They're playing our game in Devon, PA!" I was absolutely flabbergasted.

I babbled on almost incoherently and with great excitement: "And look at this…there's an International Frisbee Association, and people are doing Frisbee stuff all over the country! We

1. *IFA Newsletter,* Vol. 1, Number 14, "Fast Flights," page 2.

are not alone; there are more people like us!" It was a huge awakening. I was incredulous. I couldn't believe that there was an International Frisbee Association, and other people actually playing Frisbee golf like we were! When I calmed down a bit, I told our small group of Frisbee club members that we had to do a *really* big tournament the following year to find out just how many people outside of our realm were playing Frisbee Golf. I figured that it would also be an opportunity to introduce our Court Frisbee game to other Frisbee players.

In order to entice attendees, I thought that if we offered something like a brand new car as the grand prize we could attract the top Frisbee players from all over the country. I figured that probably no one had ever given away such a big prize for a Frisbee competition before.

So from that moment on, I started planning for a big Frisbee Golf tournament to be held in August 1974. I had been accused of dreaming big in the past, but now my buddies really thought I was crazy. "How are you going to get a brand new car to give away as a prize," they exclaimed. I responded by telling them "I don't know, but I'll find a way somehow."

My optimism was based upon my thinking that giving a brand new car away at a Frisbee event would be so unique that it would surely attract the interest of businesses looking for big promotional value. I assumed that some business somewhere would jump at the chance to be a car-supplying sponsor. And where better to start than Wham-O? After all, they were the ones making and selling Frisbee discs; they would probably be thrilled to be part of a big promotion that would attract much attention to their product. Or so I thought.

I started out by writing a four-page typewritten letter to Wham-O explaining how the game of Frisbee Golf and my game of Court Frisbee, taken together, would test all the skills of Frisbee throwing. I explained how that would be a natural combination for a big tournament designed to find out who was the best overall Frisbee player in the country.

I carefully described how Frisbee Golf fully tested both distance and accuracy throwing skills; and that Court Frisbee tested pinpoint accuracy as well as adroit catching skills and athletic attributes of timing and quick reflexes. I pointed out that the uniqueness of a Frisbee competition of this type would attract the attention of a huge number of people. I told them that if people heard that a brand new car was going to be given away to the person who could prove that he or she was the best Frisbee thrower in the nation, they would naturally want to attend to see what the event was all about. I felt sure that Wham-O would see it that way also, so I concluded the letter with a proposal that they donate the car in exchange for being the title-sponsor of the event, which I was planning to call the "United States Frisbee Championship."

As I dropped the letter into the mailbox, I imagined the response that I would get back. "Dear Mr. Palmeri, What a great idea! A unique event like that would turn thousands of people on to the joys and pleasures of Frisbee throwing. It would be a great promotion for our Frisbee product. We would be glad to be the sponsor of the event and to donate the car to be given to the winner. We will donate all the Frisbee discs you need for the competition as well. Please keep us informed of your needs."

Yeah, right…dream on, Jim, dream on….

I was ecstatic when I received a quick reply, but was somewhat surprised to find it sent by Harvey J. Kukuk, the director of the International Frisbee Association, instead of the Wham-O Manufacturing Company to which I had sent my proposal. I didn't know at the time that the IFA was not a separate entity, but just a promotional organization run by Wham-O. I also didn't know that Harvey J. Kukuk was just a fictional character created as part of the zaniness with which the IFA was being promoted. I figured that Wham-O had forwarded my letter to the IFA. Regardless, I was extremely disappointed in what good old Harvey J. wrote.

He thanked me for my interest in Frisbee, but told me the tournament I proposed was not within the scope of activities that Wham-O was interested in at this time. Harvey wrote that the word "Frisbee" was a registered trademark of Wham-O, and that if I were to hold the tournament I proposed, I could not use the word "Frisbee" as part of the name of the event or for its promotion. Furthermore, I was told that failure to comply with that request would result in legal proceedings.

I was shocked at what I was reading, and for a brief moment my enthusiasm and resolve for all things Frisbee wavered. But I still had a strong belief that a big tournament to showcase playing golf with a Frisbee disc could be a huge success and a great promotion for some sponsor, somewhere. My determination quickly returned, and I resolved to forge ahead with my idea without the help of Wham-O. I replied to Harvey J. Kukuk telling him that I was disappointed in Wham-O's response, but that I would change the name of my event to the American Flying Disc Open, and would refer to the "Frisbee" Golf event as "Flying Disc Golf." I also asked Harvey to inform Wham-O that I would seek other sponsors.

So seek I did, with very little success at first. But after much searching around, going door to door to car dealers in Rochester, I found one automobile dealer that was somewhat interested in getting involved. They stopped far short of donating the car, but did offer to provide a brand new Datsun B210 at their cost. I was getting desperate by that time, but was convinced that I could raise the money to cover the cost of the car. So I accepted their offer and went forward with my plans for the big tournament. I was going to do whatever I could to make the American Flying Disc Open happen.

My next step was to send out a somewhat formal news release to the ten largest newspapers around the country, to *Sports Illustrated,* and to Harvey J. Kukuk of the IFA. (I still had no clue that Harvey J. Kukuk was a totally fictional character and that Wham-O was running the IFA show and writing its newsletter.)

I got no responses from any of the newspapers or from *Sports Illustrated,* but the IFA *did* put this note in their "Frisbee Datelines" section of the next issue of the *IFA Newsletter*:

> The Rochester Frisbee Club has developed a new game called Court Frisbee which it believes may be the answer to a universal form of competition for Frisbee players. Anyone who would like details on the game can contact Jim Palmeri (#65,400), 153 Susan Lane, Rochester, NY 14616. They are interested in hosting a national event in August and welcome all inquiries.

It is interesting to note that, while Court Frisbee was only one part of the tournament, they completely ignored the fact that Flying Disc Golf was the primary event.

At any rate, I proceeded with an all-consuming effort to make the American Flying Disc Open a big tournament that would attract the attention of the best Frisbee throwers in the nation, and hopefully make Wham-O see that they missed the boat.

The car dealer Pacesetter Motors of Rochester, New York, actively helped me with a lot of the tournament details. They saw the opportunity to get some publicity out of the event and were anxious to see things done right. The first thing they did was to plan a photo shoot of them presenting me with the new car. This photo was used in a press release in which there was no mention that I was paying for the car...just that they were "providing" a brand new Datsun B-210 as the prize for the upcoming American Flying Disc Open. (They did, in the end, decide to provide the car somewhat below their cost, saving a couple of hundred dollars off what I originally thought I was going to have to raise from the entry fees, spectator fees, tournament concessions, and other sponsors.) I really thought that people would be so curious about someone winning a car by playing Frisbee that they would flock by the thousands to see the event. At a dollar per spectator entry, the car was as good as donated! So I thought....

I sent that photo to Harvey J. at the IFA, and was surprised to get a phone call from a Wham-O executive named Irv Lander. I found out later that Irv was the Major Promotions and Publicity Director with Wham-O, and the photo I sent to Harvey J. had gone directly to him! The photo of the car being presented to me may have made Wham-O realize that I was serious and perhaps they began to see some promotional value in what I was doing after all. Regardless of what they were thinking, they put a blurb (right) in the *IFA Newsletter* that came out in the spring of 1974, but they again did not mention anything about Flying Disc Golf being featured in the tournament!

ROCHESTER, N.Y.—Jim Palmeri (65400) of the Rochester Frisbee Club has arranged for a 1974 Datsun to be given to the winner of the upcoming American Flying Disc Open.

Jim, (L), accepts the car from car dealer **Tony Simonetti**.

However, the phone call I received from Irv Lander wasn't so positive. Irv said that he was concerned that I was getting in over my head and that I should start with a small local event to gain experience. He said that after a couple of years at that level, Wham-O might be glad to work with me on a bigger event. I calmly informed him I had already done that kind of thing. I told him that I had organized a small tournament four years ago, another tournament three years ago, and that I followed up by running two consecutive City of Rochester championship events over the past two years for a total of four years of experience, including organizing weekly league play for the Rochester Frisbee Club members over the past two years. I told Irv that I was ready to do a big tournament now, and was prepared to go ahead with my plans. It was at that point that Irv Lander said that Wham-O would like to help out, and would send me a case of Wham-O Pro Models for the competitors to use at the event. Not quite the car I had hoped they would provide, but a case of Frisbee discs was better than nothing.

The big American Flying Disc Open tournament that I envisioned came together on the weekend of August 4–5, 1974 at St. John Fisher College in Rochester. However, despite great local press and TV promos, the thousands of spectators that I expected actually turned out to be fewer than twenty people! The $1.00 spectator fee I charged did *not* cover the cost of the car.

Financially, the event was a big washout, but I was absolutely correct about one thing: giving a car away to the winner accomplished the goal of getting some of the very best Frisbee players in the land to come to Rochester to compete in the tournament. Twenty-eight local players and thirty-four players from all corners of the nation came to vie for the new car.

John Kirkland, one of the biggest names in Frisbee at that time, came from Boston; Victor Malafronte, perhaps the biggest name in Frisbee, came from California. Dan "Stork" Roddick showed up with a large New Jersey contingent including Irv Kalb, Bob "Flash" Kingsley, and the late-great Gary Seubert. John Connelly and Tom Cleworth, the core of the highly regarded Chicago-based Highland Avenue Aces Guts team came to try to claim the new car. Fellow Chicagoan Bruce Koger also made the trek to Rochester. John Sappington and Scott Dickson from Ann Arbor, Michigan showed up with John and Jo Cahow, two other players from their Humblies Guts team. Jo was the only woman player to enter the tournament, and would go on to humble many of the guys in the days to come. Kerry Kollmar and Mark Danna drove up with a small group from New York City. Craig Lattimer arrived from Erie, Pennsylvania; and John Schaberg came from Devon, Pennsylvania with his raccoon. Buffalo, New York delivered up Mike Jackman and Mark Schumacher. Star Ultimate players Mike Whelan and Bob Evans from Princeton University showed up. Geoff Hungerford made a point of coming from Colorado to participate. (Geoff was a former Rochester native and he wanted to match his skills with former high school classmate Doug Corea.)

In all, sixty-two competitors showed up; the player list looked like a cross section of what would have been a Who's Who of the best Frisbee players in the nation back then. This also included some totally unknown Frisbee players; twenty-eight of them were from Rochester and were people even the members of the Rochester Frisbee Club had never seen or heard of before! Guys like Ted Naylon, Dave Marini, Woody Michaels, and Jim "Gus" Emerson were flushed out of the woodwork by the promise of winning the Datsun. These guys hadn't heard of the Rochester Frisbee Club despite two previous City of Rochester Frisbee Championships. Most of them hadn't even heard of, or known each other! Back in 1974, isolated pockets of Frisbee play weren't just regional—they existed right in your own backyard.

Please understand that at that time, the players in any given area of local play didn't really know how skillful Frisbee players elsewhere were. The only frame of reference a Frisbee player had to judge his own skills was the other players in his little local community.

So when you heard about a brand-new car being given away to the best Frisbee player in a tournament, and you were the best Frisbee player in your little group, you naturally thought you had a great chance to win that car. And many individuals really didn't even have a group...like Ted Naylon. They just enjoyed flipping a Frisbee with a few friends now and then, and were considerably better than their friends were at the basic skills. They had never heard of Frisbee Golf before, but could throw farther and more accurately than their friends could. They all basically thought that the car was as good as theirs. I know what Ted Naylon had to be thinking: "Hey if this jerk wants to give me a car, I am going to take him up on it!" I bet Victor Malafronte and John Kirkland were thinking the very same thing.

That type of thinking applied to most every one of the sixty-two players who signed up for the tournament. Well over half of them had never played Frisbee Golf before, but they all were at or near the top of their particular Frisbee group in throwing skills, and thought that they had a great chance to take home the big prize.

I had my own dreams of glory by the same principle. I had always been considered top dog in the Rochester Frisbee Club, but late-comer Doug Corea joined our club just three months before the tournament and dashed my hopes. No one locally had ever thrown a Frisbee as far as Doug could throw one. No one could throw a Frisbee more accurately than Doug for that matter. And no one had ever beaten him in a round of Frisbee Golf. He was a shoe-in to win the car as far as we were concerned. We just couldn't imagine how anyone could beat him, especially since he helped to set up the course at the St. John Fisher College tournament site, and knew it inside and out.

But even Doug was surprised when Bruce Koger showed up a couple of days early to practice the course. Bruce pumped the disc farther than any of us had ever seen a Frisbee fly, even farther than Doug's best throws. As the other big names of Frisbee rolled into town, the same scenario played out over again. Kirkland, Malafronte, and the Michigan and Chicago Guts Frisbee guys flew their Frisbees as far or even farther than Bruce Koger could. It was mind blowing! And these guys were among the few players who did have experience at playing Frisbee Golf.

As the players warmed up and practiced the course on Friday, August 3, 1974, they began to observe that, even though they were either the best or nearly the best Frisbee players in their own little sphere of Frisbee playing, many of the other competitors were as good, if not better, than they were. They began to realize that winning the car was not going to be the cakewalk they thought it was going to be.

Other than the regular Rochester Frisbee Club members, those few competitors who did happen to have previous experience with Frisbee Golf had never holed out by putting into a receptacle-type target similar to what the Rochester Frisbee Club members had been using. The six-inch high, two-foot-square cardboard box that was our standard Frisbee Golf hole required a very different putting style than what they had practiced with their targets back home.

Frisbee Golf to them meant that the "hole" was a specified object to be hit with a disc: a tree trunk, telephone pole, park bench, statue, or any other suitable object along their course.

Object Frisbee Golf was a nearly universal concept for anyone playing the game prior to 1974. There may have been some exceptions somewhere, but other than the local Rochester Frisbee Club members, none of the participants who came to the AFDO had putted into hole-like containers...and they were *very* uncomfortable putting into our little boxes. A few even strongly argued that we shouldn't use the boxes, that we should change the setup and designate tree trunks and light poles for putting. But I certainly wasn't going to abandon my carefully

The prototype of the standard two foot square box "hole" that was used at the 1974 AFDO.

planned holes, or the boxes, just because some people didn't like our concept of putting. I was as uncomfortable at the thought of hitting objects as they were of using my little boxes!

Despite the putting controversy, the very best Frisbee players in the tournament were still confident that they would prevail. Most of them had been playing Frisbee since the late sixties, and that is why they were among the best. However, none of them were aware of the skills and prowess of Dan "Stork" Roddick. They weren't aware that he had been playing Frisbee much longer than any other active Frisbee player anywhere in the world, except perhaps his dad, Papa Jack Roddick, who also showed up to play in the AFDO. Jack and Dan had started honing their disc-flying skills back in the early 1950s. Dan's accuracy off the tee and his up shots were impeccable. Despite only previously putting by hitting designated objects, he seemed able to adapt to putting into a little box faster than the rest of the field. His three-round Flying Disc Golf score was eleven throws ahead of Tom Cleworth in 2nd place, and twelve throws ahead of Victor Malafronte in 3rd place.

The top 10 Scores for the 3 Rounds of Flying Disc Golf:

Rank	Player	Scores	Points earned
1st	Dan Roddick, Piscataway, NJ	56-59-59=174	40
2nd	Tom Cleworth, Wilmette IL	64-59-62=185	39
3rd	Victor Malafronte, Berkeley, CA	64-59-63=186	38
T-4th	John Kirkland, Boston, MA	66-63-58=187	36
T-4th	Mark Danna, NYC	62-66-59=187	36
T-4th	Doug Corea, Rochester, NY	64-62-61=187	36
T-7th	John Connelly, Wilmette, IL	65-65-63=193	33
T-7th	Bruce Koger, Chicago, IL	70-63-60=193	33
T-7th	Jack McGill, Mikado, MI	66-65-62=193	33
10th	Kerry Kollmar, NYC	69-60-66=194	31

It turned out that my original assessment of Doug Corea wasn't too far off the pace. In the Flying Disc Golf portion of the tournament, he finished tied with John Kirkland and Mark Danna for 4th place. Doug slipped up a bit in the Court Frisbee side of the tournament, and finished 7th place overall. Not bad for a local Rochester guy considering some of the superstars of Frisbee that he had to go up against—guys he never even knew existed before that weekend.

The Datsun B-210 was awarded on the basis of the total points scored in both the golf event and the Court Frisbee event. Points were awarded to the top 40 finishers from the golf round in the reverse order of finish—first place got 40 points, second got 39 points, down to 1 point for the 40th place finisher. The top 40 Frisbee golfers qualified to compete in the Court Frisbee round of competition, where they were awarded points for their order of finish on the same basis as the points awarded in the Frisbee Golf event.

The Top Ten From the Court Frisbee (DDC) Competition:

Rank	Player	Points Earned
1st	John Kirkland, Boston, MA	40
2nd	Mark Danna, NYC	39
3rd	Dan Roddick, Piscataway, NJ	38
4th	Kerry Kollmar, NYC	37
5th	John Connelly, Wilmette, IL	36
6th	Craig Lattimer, Fairview, PA	35
7th	Jimmy Scala, Somerville, NJ	34
8th	John Rzepka, Rochester, NY	33
9th	Tom Cleworth, Wilmette IL	32
10th	Doug Corea, Rochester, NY	31

When the points from both events were combined, the overall top ten finishers in the tournament were:

Top Ten Finishers in the Tournament:

Rank	Player	DG Points	DDC Points	Total Points
1st	Dan Roddick, Piscataway, NJ	40	38	78
2nd	John Kirkland, Boston, MA	36	40	76
3rd	Mark Danna, NYC	36	39	75
4th	Tom Cleworth, Wilmette IL	39	32	71
5th	John Connelly, Wilmette, IL	33	36	69
6th	Kerry Kollmar, NYC	31	37	68
7th	Doug Corea, Rochester, NY	36	31	67
8th	Craig Lattimer, Fairview, PA	30	35	65
9th	Irv Kalb, South Orange, NJ	28	30	58
10th	Jimmy Scala, Somerville, NJ	23.5	34	57.5

Dan Roddick had already been known in Frisbee circles as an ardent Frisbee enthusiast. His collaboration with Flash Kingsley in creating the *Flying Disc World* newsletter bolstered his standing in the IFA-based Frisbee community of that time. He also had a reputation as a strong player in the fledgling Ultimate culture that was beginning to boom in 1974. He was a key figure on the undefeated and highly regarded Rutgers Ultimate team.

And now, with his victory over the very top Frisbee players in the world in their quest for a new car, his standing as a great all-around Frisbee player rose right to the top of the list.

Dan's victory in the original AFDO tournament turned out to be a key factor that prompted the transformation of Frisbee Golf from an occasionally played activity in unrelated pockets scattered all over the country, into the unified, well-organized competitive sport of Disc Golf that we know today.

Jim Palmeri hands Dan "Stork" Roddick the keys to the Datsun after his victory in the 1974 American Flying Disc Open in Rochester, NY.

Chapter 7

A Chain of Events

The Sport Gets its Foundation

SOMETHING I DIDN'T KNOW ABOUT at the time I was planning the American Flying Disc Open was that Wham-O —with Ed Headrick at the helm—had been working hard on a super big tournament of their own, and it was scheduled for just three weeks after my August 3–4 AFDO. It was not publicized in the *IFA Newsletter* because it was a special invitational event designed to gather the very top Frisbee players from around the country, and show them off in Pasadena's Rose Bowl as a major marketing promotion for the Frisbee.

This mega-event was designed to introduce the new World Class Frisbee Master title that the IFA was planning to confer upon those who could pass its stringent Frisbee skills test. Wham-O had put together a list of superior Frisbee players who were recognized as the leaders in the Guts and Ultimate communities, plus a few at-large Frisbee players who had made a noteworthy name for themselves through their dedicated Frisbee play. The invited players were generally considered to be the elite of the Frisbee scene of that time. The invitees got an all-expense-paid trip to Pasadena for one week of Frisbee play, and a big showcase finale in the

Rose Bowl in front of all kinds of news media and a crowd of 20,000 spectators.

It was one of the main reasons that Wham-O had tried to get me to back away from my AFDO. They were putting a lot of time and energy into their enormous Rose Bowl extravaganza, and did not want any distractions to take away from their efforts. I didn't know about this upcoming World Frisbee Championships (WFC) event at that time, and only found out about it at the AFDO because all of the important Frisbee players who had come to my tournament had already been invited to the upcoming WFC. At some point during the AFDO weekend, the subject of the looming WFC came up, and most of the Rose Bowl invitees thought I had also been invited. Some assumed I had an in with Wham-O since I had been at Dan Roddick's Octad meet in May of that year. Others assumed that anyone putting up a car for a sizable Frisbee tournament must have been a Wham-O insider, and that they just hadn't heard of me yet. A few of the biggest names, super Wham-O V.I.P. Victor Malafronte in particular, said that they were going to talk to Wham-O and see if they could get me an invitation. But they didn't realize that not only was I not a Wham-O insider, I was considered to be a Wham-O nemesis, mainly because I didn't take their advice and stick to a small local tournament with normal trophies as prizes. They were also disgruntled because I allowed the use of other flying disc brands in my tournament. Dan Roddick was almost denied an invitation for the same reason. His Octad also permitted the use of any brand of flying discs and Wham-O was not happy about that. But Dan's long-standing association with Wham-O, and longtime advocacy and promotion of Frisbee play, made them overlook that factor in his case, and he was invited to their big event nevertheless.

Since a large block of the invitees to the 1974 Rose Bowl WFC had attended the AFDO, there was plenty of banter among the WFC participants about the AFDO, winning a new car, Disc Golf in general, and about Octad. All this talk did not go unnoticed by Ed Headrick. It made him begin to do some serious thinking about possible directions that Wham-O might take in promoting their Frisbee products. The wheels were in motion; big changes to the tenor of the Frisbee community were in store.

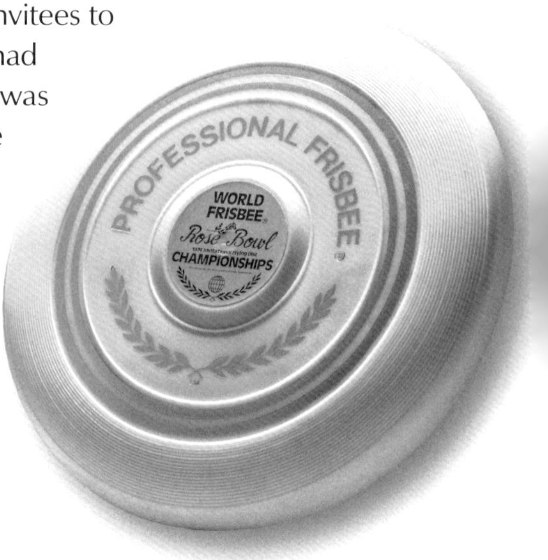

Commemorative Pro with front and back labels given to players at the 1974 Rose Bowl WFC

One of the first assessments that Ed Headrick made from the activities of 1974 was that the frivolity of the Harvey J. Kukuk era of the IFA didn't match the more serious sports-minded competitiveness and dedicated approach the current Frisbee players were taking. Ed took into account Flash Kingsley and Dan Roddick's *Flying Disc World* newsletter. The difference between its straightforward talk about competitive disc sports, and the *IFA Newsletter's* lighthearted chatter about Frisbee and Harvey's Aardvark hunting was as night and day as you could get.

After the 1974 WFC was over, Ed began to wonder about the changing times and did some research. One of the things he did was to experiment with Disc Golf at Oak Grove Park in

La Cañada, California near his home. He designated specific light poles as targets to hit, and selected certain landmarks in the park to tee from. We don't know how often Ed experimented that fall, and perhaps during the spring of 1975, but it did signal a change of attitude in his concept of Disc Golf.

Ed's investigation into Disc Golf was at least partly due to all of the hoopla surrounding the emergence of Disc Golf competition that took place in 1974—including the car given away at AFDO. Also giving him pause was the seemingly inexplicable drawing power that Disc Golf had on many players. Dan Roddick, Gary Seubert, and Flash Kingsley had followed up their 1974 spring Octad event with a season-ending October event called the "Jersey Jam" which featured a Disc Golf tournament along with an experimental judged Freestyle event. Ed couldn't help but notice how many of the top name Frisbee players made the effort to attend what seemed like a small-scale, local event. He probably figured that if the *Flying Disc World* newsletter was being taken seriously by enough players to travel all the way to New Jersey from Boston, Michigan, California, and other far-flung places around the country, then something was up.

Whatever Ed figured at that time, he made a decision to work with Dan Roddick and Flash Kingsley on their upcoming second Annual Octad tournament—planned for the 1975 Memorial Day weekend. He authorized the creation of a special version of the Super Pro Frisbee with an Octad 1975 hot stamp design. Each competitor who registered for the 1975 Octad was given one of these commemorative discs, which became an instant collector's item.

Ed Headrick personally attended the 1975 Octad, not only to give promotional support, but to check out just what this new wave of competitive Frisbee activity was all about. The Octad, AFDO, and Jersey Jam of 1974 had taken Ed by surprise, and now he wanted to observe this new direction of Frisbee activity firsthand.

The 1975 "Octad" Super Pro

A significant observation Ed made was how enthusiastic and receptive the players were about the Disc Golf event. For many of the sixty-five competitors who entered the 1975 Octad, this was the first time they competed in any of the eight events. Some of the players declined to try the Discathon event and the two Self-Caught Flight (SCF) events, but virtually all the players enthusiastically entered the Disc Golf event, including the ones who had never played it before. Disc Golf didn't intimidate the newcomers as much as the more technical SCF events or the rigorous Discathon event did. Astute Ed Headrick noticed little things like that, and he took it all in.

The 1975 Octad Disc Golf event was played on the Johnson Park Disc Golf course that Dan Roddick, Gary Seubert, and Flash Kingsley had laid out specifically for their Jersey Jam Disc Golf event the previous October. It was one of the earliest Disc Golf courses to be designed as a semi-permanent course in which the same hole placements and tee areas were mapped out and reused. Johnson Park was subsequently the venue for local, regional, and national Disc Golf events held in the Rutgers University area for many years.

The Johnson Park course featured the modified "Seubert Basket" Disc Golf hole. Gary had first introduced his basket-hole concept at the 1974 Jersey Jam. They had been inspired by the little six-inch high by two-foot square box targets used at the 1974 AFDO, but were much bigger. They were four feet in diameter and fifteen inches deep. Apparently Gary was not happy with how many of his putts at the AFDO bounced out of the tiny two-foot-square boxes that were only six inches high. That wasn't a problem with his relatively cavernous Jersey Jam baskets—virtually any time a disc landed in one of those holes, it stayed in.

But after the Jersey Jam Disc Golf event was over, a consensus of the players felt that the baskets were *too* big, and did not present enough of a putting challenge. Gary modified his basket design accordingly and introduced his new two-and-a-half-foot diameter, ten-inch-high baskets at the 1975 Octad. They were actually great putting targets and became the de facto standard before the chained Disc Pole Hole baskets were invented.

It was at the 1975 Octad that Ed Headrick first observed a putting concept other than throwing though a vertical Hula Hoop, or hitting telephone or light poles, or other designated objects. And he saw something he distinctly did *not* like.

While watching the finals of the 1975 Octad Disc Golf event I happened to be standing right next to Ed Headrick. He was keenly interested in the nature of the game. At one point, Ed observed a player preparing to execute a putt of about 25 feet. The player held the disc vertically to the ground and launched

Jim Challas shown putting to an early ground basket on hole 18 at the 1976 NAS tournament in Amherst, Massachusetts.

it with a high up-and-down trajectory. This was known among the few disc golfers who had previously used the box or basket-type targets as the "vertical putt." Upon seeing that putt, Ed gruffly exclaimed, "That's disgusting!...A Frisbee isn't meant to fly like that!" He held strong opinions as to just what the flight of the Frisbee was supposed to be like. "Flat Flip Flies Straight, Tilted Flip Curves." But vertical putt? No way! Ed Headrick became very much disenchanted with putting into a ground basket.

Regardless, it was clear that Disc Golf was on Ed's mind at that point. So much so that when I wrote Wham-O to see if they would help out with the second annual AFDO I was planning that summer, I didn't get any of the Harvey J. Kukuk nonsense.

They even offered to supply several cases of Wham-O Pro Models for the competitors to use. But far more importantly, Ed sent his top three Wham-O executives to Rochester to compete in the 1975 AFDO: Bob Gardner, Vice President of Operations; Wally Schneider, Vice-President of Sales; and Ernie Wilkerson, Vice President of Premium Products (Mr. Fastback Frisbee himself). Ed wanted to gather more information and opinions about the rapidly growing interest in Disc Golf competition that was popping up all over.

I don't know what Wally Schneider thought about Disc Golf, but I do know that Ernie Wilkerson was having a great time and that Bob Gardner was bubbling over with excitement about what he experienced at the 1975 AFDO. That was the first year that Ellison Park had been used for Disc Golf. The Ellison Park Disc Golf course was a standout course even by today's standards. The course was a wondrous facility that had no comparison anywhere. Bob Gardner just loved it, and although I don't know the details of the feedback he gave to Ed Headrick, I know it must have been very positive because of the ease with which George Sappenfield and Dan Roddick convinced Ed that Disc Golf should be a part of the second annual Rose Bowl WFC Wham-O was planning for later that summer.

George had been hired as a consultant back in 1969, and had always advocated that Disc Golf was a great way to promote the Frisbee disc. But that was one subject about which Wham-O just didn't take his advice, and continued to ignore the game… until 1975, that is. After the Disc Golf events of 1974 and 1975, Ed Headrick started to seriously reassess the concept of Disc Golf. I wonder if George ever gave Ed a good dose of "I told you so."

At any rate, it didn't take much to convince Ed that Disc Golf should be a part of the 1975 WFC. Ed was ready to go. I personally don't think Ed really needed to be convinced at that point. I really think he was just looking for corroboration that the idea to include Disc Golf was a good one, and wouldn't be a mistake. After making the decision to add Disc Golf to the 1975 WFC, Ed personally designed the Disc Golf course to be used. He decided that nearby Oak Grove Park would be a good place for the course.[1] The installation was finished barely two weeks before the invited competitors arrived for the second annual WFC. Ed designated tee areas by installing professional-looking tee signs. For putting targets, he installed four-foot-high, two-inch-diameter poles in the ground. Hitting the pole with a disc constituted a successful putt. Ed hated the vertical putt and wanted nothing to do with the ground baskets that encouraged them. His poles in the ground successfully eliminated any chance the vertical putt would be used at his first Disc Golf course.

The Frisbee players invited to the 1975 WFC could be classified into three categories:

1. Those who had never seen or played Disc Golf before. They didn't have any putting concept to compare with the hit-the-pole type of putting.

2. Those who had played the game now and then but had never putted into ground baskets. This group was the most accepting of the hit-the-pole concept.

3. The few Frisbee players who had been actively competing in Disc Golf for the past year or two, almost always putting into

1. More info on the Oak Grove course coming up in Chapter 8.

ground baskets which had already become their standard for Disc Golf competition. This group distinctly disliked the hit-the-pole putting concept.

Regardless of the Disc Golf background the players had, the overall feedback that Ed got about the hitting-the-pole concept of putting was a bit negative. The main complaint was that it just wasn't definitive enough whether a close putt actually hit the pole or not. A player would react to a long putt that came extremely close to the pole with an exclamation of "It hit!" The competitors might retort "No it didn't, I didn't hear any ping!" The same sort of thing applied to a long upshot around a

One of the original metal pole "holes" in Oak Grove Park, La Cañada, CA. Irv Kalb putting in the 1975 WFC Disc Golf event with Jimmy Scala observing whether or not the disc actually hits the pole. Dan "Stork" Roddick and Jim Palmeri looking on.

blind corner. As the players came into view of the pole and saw a disc laying several inches from it, they didn't know whether it had hit the pole and bounced off, or stopped inches short of sliding into the pole. Furthermore, the Disc Golf portion of Oak Grove Park had a desert-like ambiance with a host of small stones and rocks lying around. Little stones often created a pinging sound when deflected against the pole by a disc landing nearby. Disagreements and ensuing arguments sometimes arose as to whether or not the disc actually hit the pole.

Ed listened to the comments, went back to the drawing board, and worked on ways to address the problems with the pole target. He was open to any solution that discouraged the use of the vertical putt he so disliked.

One possible reason for Ed's attitude toward the vertical putt is his background with the Frisbee. Upon beginning his career at Wham-O in 1964, Ed had a marketing vision for the Frisbee. He wanted to move away from the perception of the Pluto Platter as being "just a kid's toy," and give it an image that fit the growing interest in physical-fitness activities and sports participation of the mid-1960s.

Ed strongly believed that the graceful and intriguing manner with which the Frisbee flew through the air was an important factor in its marketability. His first step was to retool the Pluto Platter mold into the Pro Model design, which gave the Frisbee a look and feel that would encourage more teenagers and adults to buy and use Frisbee discs. His reasoning was basic: if more people bought and used their Frisbee products, more people would become enamored with their intriguing flight and discover the fun of the Frisbee. This would escalate sales and the products would be successful. Ed's discovery of the Healy brothers and their annual International Frisbee Tournament activities corroborated his reasoning and helped him convince the owners of Wham-O that they should stay the course and keep Frisbee discs in their line of products. Between the successful promotion of the IFT and the adoption of the Healy brothers' International Frisbee Association idea, Frisbee sales began to grow steadily. Ed's next and highly astute step was to begin the *IFA Newsletter* promotion in 1968. This may have been the single most important event that stimulated the development of the Frisbee culture and the development of disc sports. The underlying foundation for all this was the intriguing flight of the Frisbee...and Ed was its guardian. His perception of how a Frisbee was meant to fly was sacrosanct. The vertical putt just did not fit into any part of Ed's perception of how a disc should fly. He felt strongly that the game of golf as played with flying discs was best served by hitting a pole-like target utilizing the primary flight characteristics of the Frisbee disc...not by plopping it into a basket with a non-aerodynamic vertical putt.

Ed's simple pole in the ground accomplished that goal, but the aforementioned objections needed to be resolved. Based on comments and recommendations garnered from the 1975 WFC Disc Golf event, the first thing he tried was to paint a marker line halfway up the pole to designate the upper portion as the putting target. A disc hitting above the marker line would be a good putt, and below was considered a missed putt.

This eliminated the uncertainty of a disc sliding near the base of the pole causing small stones to create the ping sound that might be interpreted as the disc hitting the pole. However, it did not solve the problem of a putt coming so close to the marked-off portion of the pole that it was impossible to determine if the disc made contact with it or not.

It took Ed the better part of a year of research and development to come up with his successful chained Disc Pole Hole solution. The problem of whether a close putt actually hit the pole or just missed was totally eliminated. The Disc Pole Hole design successfully preserved the intent of hitting an object to simulate a putt, and still rendered the vertical putt useless. Ed's original Disc Pole Hole introduced some new problems, but constant tinkering and design modifications helped to minimize those problems to a somewhat acceptable level.

The bottom line was that Ed Headrick's desire to create a standardized putting target that would also preserve his notion of the proper flight of the Frisbee disc led to the invention of the chained Disc Pole Hole. Ed installed them at the Oak Grove and La Mirada courses in the L.A. area during the summer of 1976. This was just in time for the 1976 World Frisbee Championships where a large portion of the world's best Frisbee athletes had the opportunity to check out the new DGA Disc Pole Holes for the first time.

The Disc Pole Hole soon began to replace ground baskets. Wherever a permanent Disc Golf course with DGA Disc Pole Holes was installed, there was no further need for the local disc golfers to use ground baskets.

Ed Headrick originally designed Disc Pole Holes with only 10 chains. This is the third one produced. Photo courtesy of Dan "Stork" Roddick.

CHAPTER 8

A CHAIN OF EVENTS

The Sport of Disc Golf Tees Off

ONE OF THE MOST IMPORTANT FIGURES in the origin of the sport of Disc Golf is Dan "Stork" Roddick. As far as we know, of all people who are currently playing Disc Golf or any other Frisbee activity, Dan Roddick started tossing a disc earlier than anyone else.

A young Stork catches his Flyin Saucer around 1956

Dan's father, "Papa" Jack Roddick, gave little five-year-old Danny a Fred Morrison-designed Flyin Saucer for Christmas in 1953.

That Flyin Saucer was soon an important part of their regular family fun activities. Papa Jack and Dan became quite proficient with fancy throws and catches—so much so that at the 1962 Seattle World's Fair, they were invited to participate with the Wham-O Frisbee Disc demonstration team. Then, three years later at the New York World's Fair, Dan and

Papa Jack again linked up with the Wham-O Frisbee team, and were actually more advanced with their throwing and catching skills than the demo team itself!

Dan attended Millersville State College in Pennsylvania from 1966 to 1970, and organized Frisbee activities on campus in between his participation on the Millersville championship-level tennis team. He also set up a Pennsylvania State Frisbee tournament during his years at Millersville, which further helped hone his Frisbee playing and organizational skills.

BENDING AT IMPACT, Frisbee is caught in skillful manner by Dan Roddick, 20, of Millersville, Pa., during Chautauqua Tournament. A similar event is planned for later in this year by members of the group which headquarters at Millersville State College.

A blurb in the* IFA Newsletter, *Vol. 1, No. 4 from 1969

When Dan went on to graduate school at Rutgers University, his prowess with a flying disc, combined with his 6′ 5″ height and basketball experience, earned him a starring role on the original Rutgers Ultimate team. He was instrumental in their victory over Princeton in the first-ever intercollegiate Ultimate game, held on November 6, 1972.

Dan attended the 1973 IFT, where he made the acquaintance of many of the top-level players of the growing Frisbee culture. One of the people he met was Bob "Flash" Kingsley, who was also attending the IFT for the first time. Bob had been playing Frisbee for almost as long as Dan. Flash had discovered the concept of Frisbee Golf early on, and shared his ideas about it with Dan. It turned out that their common interest in Frisbee led to Dan offering Flash a job at Rutgers University where Dan was working while studying toward his PhD in Sociology.

The first thing they did together was to start up the *Flying Disc World* newsletter, which as far as we know was the first independently published national newsletter about disc sports. It took an informative and serious view of competitive flying disc activities and was well received by the small but growing number of Frisbee players who were actively competing in Guts, Ultimate, and Frisbee Golf.

In conjunction with their newsletter, Dan and Flash teamed up with Gary Seubert, a local Frisbee enthusiast, to promote the Octad (named because it consisted of eight different flying disc events, including Disc Golf). It was scheduled for the first weekend in May of 1974, and was the first nationally promoted, overall type of tournament of its kind. It attracted a small but hard-core group of Frisbee players from all around the country, plus a small number of obscure but equally enthusiastic Frisbee players who were active in the local New Brunswick/Piscataway, New Jersey-area Ultimate community.

Dan Roddick had already been on Wham-O's "watch list" due to his previous accomplishments, but after publishing *Flying Disc World*, organizing Octad, and winning the car at the 1974 AFDO, Dan was at or near the top of the list of people they were keeping an eye on. This visibility led to Dan's invitation to the inaugural WFC in 1974. Then when Dan promoted a second annual Octad in the spring of 1975, and participated in the hallowed IFT that summer, Wham-O decided that he would be perfect for the newly created Sports Promotion Director position they were looking to fill. Wham-O had created this position in response to the rapidly growing interest in disc sports that was taking place in 1974. They offered Dan the position, and he accepted.

Ed Headrick's primary objectives for this new position were to revamp the nature of the International Frisbee Association, and to convert the old *IFA Newsletter* into a full-blown magazine with factual content to replace the humorous tone of the old newsletter. Harvey J. Kukuk and all of the other quirky nonsense that once served Wham-O's promotional purposes were out. The new magazine, *Frisbee World*, with its straight-forward coverage of Frisbee sports, tournament schedules, disc-throwing instructional articles, and event results was in.

One of Stork's first tasks in his new position was to help organize, plan, and direct the upcoming second annual WFC. Dan and George Sappenfield helped Ed Headrick come to the conclusion that Disc Golf should be included as one of the events. Once that decision was final, Ed started the process of getting a Disc Golf course ready to be used for the 1975 WFC.

He favored Oak Grove Park in La Cañada, California as the venue for the Disc Golf competition and asked the Parks and Recreation Department for permission to use a section of the park for that purpose. Ed Headrick lived near the park and he knew the

Jimmy Scala's leaping split at the '75 WFC inspired the '76 NAS hotstamp.

Parks & Rec personnel quite well. Another reason for choosing Oak Grove was that it was near the athletic fields of La Cañada High School where some of the other WFC events were going to be held. Furthermore, Oak Grove Park was where Ed had first started experimenting with Disc Golf after hearing all the talk and hoopla about it during the 1974 WFC.

Parks & Rec agreed to let Wham-O set up the course for the duration of the WFC. However, the Disc Golf event generated quite a bit of interest among the local La Cañada residents, and a surprising number of people came to the park to try out the course in the days following the WFC. The park officials decided to keep the course set up for a while and monitor its usage. They were amazed at how many people played the Disc Golf course over the next few weeks. Ed Headrick also took notice. It made Ed think that just maybe George Sappenfield had been right all along about Disc Golf being a good thing for Wham-O to support. Ed became quite enthused with the concept of Disc Golf, and ideas began ruminating in his mind.

Ed suggested to the La Cañada Parks Department that they set the pole targets and tee signs into concrete and make the course a permanent recreational facility for the residents of the town. After the period of observation, the La Cañada Parks Department followed up on Ed's suggestion, and Oak Grove Park became the world's first permanent Disc Golf course.

In response to all this positive feedback about Disc Golf, Ed strongly backed Dan Roddick's proposal to include Disc Golf as an event in each of the tournaments in the national series that Dan was planning for the 1976 season. Dan had proposed this tournament series as a way of qualifying players

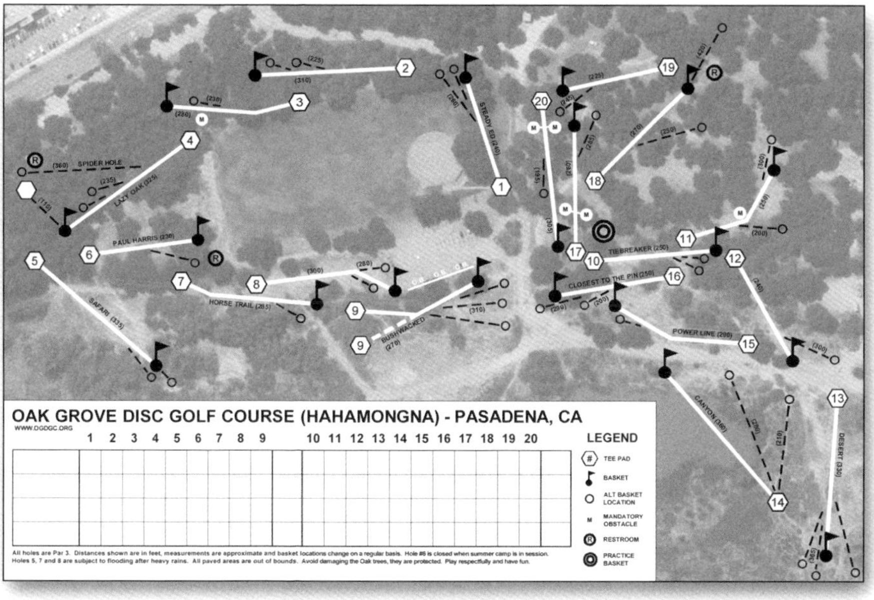

The Oak Grove Disc Golf Course as it is today

to participate in the 1976 WFC, replacing the invitation-only policy that was used to select the participants for the first two WFC Rose Bowl events. This proposed tournament series was named the "North American Series" and became known as the NAS to the Frisbee players.

Ed was astute enough to see how the Disc Golf tournaments of 1974 and 1975 had been attracting the attention and interest of Frisbee players everywhere—even those who had never known about Disc Golf previously. The favorable response the residents of La Cañada and surrounding areas had given to the Oak Grove course further reinforced Ed's thoughts about Disc Golf. He also had seen how the La Cañada Parks and Recreation Department responded favorably to the interest that people showed toward Disc Golf. He began to think that Disc Golf could be a financially sound business, and felt that there could be a market for Disc Golf courses and golf discs as the sport became more well known and visible to the public. He figured that if other cities responded to Dan Roddick's NAS Disc Golf events in the same manner that La Cañada had, they might also be interested in creating permanent Disc Golf facilities in one or more of their own local parks.

Ed Headrick made a decision and took action. He drew up a business plan based upon his assessments of how much Dan Roddick's NAS tournament series could create widespread interest in the sport. His final step was to resign from his position at Wham-O and to start up his own Disc Golf business.

Ed's astute assessment was entirely correct. The synergy between Dan's NAS qualifying tournaments and Ed's follow-up to the parks department in the cities where those tournaments were held led to an amazingly rapid growth of Disc Golf.

In that first year, 1976, many of the Frisbee enthusiasts who participated in or watched the NAS tournaments had never heard of Disc Golf before. The players who traveled to these major NAS tournaments enthusiastically took the concept back with them and started to set up local Disc Golf activity and tournaments in their own cities and towns. This activity generated the same type of interest by their local parks departments as had happened at La Cañada. This in turn generated even more leads for Ed Headrick to follow. The result was an escalating process leading to more of Ed Headrick's DGA Disc Golf courses being built.

The full account of how Ed Headrick launched his business and all that has followed is a fascinating story...which fortunately is already being written by an excellent author, Frisbee historian, and Disc Golf Hall of Fame member, Joe Feidt.

Joe's book begins right here where we leave off—as Dan Roddick took the reins of the IFA and kicked off the 1976 NAS tournament series. Joe starts out with the story of how Ed Headrick and his son, Ken, came up with the idea for the chain version of the Disc Pole Hole, and how he began selling Disc Golf courses. Joe also relates the story of Ed forming the PDGA to organize and promote the sport of Disc Golf.

Joe's book tells the story of how the PDGA evolved into the true players' organization and governing body of Disc Golf. He writes about all the people that Dan Roddick's NAS series brought together, and the blood, sweat, and tears that they expended in building this great sport of ours. Joe will talk about players like Tom Monroe, Doug Newland, Jim Powers, Jo Cahow, Ted Smethers, John Bird, Dan Mangone, Sheryl Newland, Ken Westerfield, Jim Kenner, John David, Mark Horn, Steve Slasor, Ace Mason, Patti Kunkle, Mike Conger, and many other movers and shakers who took the fledgling sport of Disc Golf and created the foundation upon which the PDGA and the huge international sport of Disc Golf was built.

Joe is a great writer and his book will complete our story. Before that, if anyone asks you where Disc Golf came from, tell them that they can read about it right from the very beginning... with this book!

Index to Appendices

The Amazing
FLYIN-SAUCER
GREAT FUN FOR THE WHOLE FAMILY!
FLYIN-SAUCER performs in an amazing way as you develop your skill in flying it. A novel way to play catch. You will think of many games to play. Adaptable to almost any game.
HOW TO FLY
Launch your FLYIN-SAUCER straight ahead with a snap of your wrist making it spin as fast as possible. DON'T THROW TOO HARD. . . . It's the spinning that gives it lift. Begin by flying about 10 feet. When windy, throw across the wind. You will quickly learn how to bank to the left or right.
FLYIN-SAUCER
(A Gyroscopic Airfoil)
PRECISELY ENGINEERED • AERODYNAMICALLY CORRECT
MADE TOUGH TO RESIST ROUGH HANDLING

The Amazing
FLYIN-SAUCER
GREAT FUN FOR THE WHOLE FAMILY!
HOW TO FLY
FLYIN-SAUCER

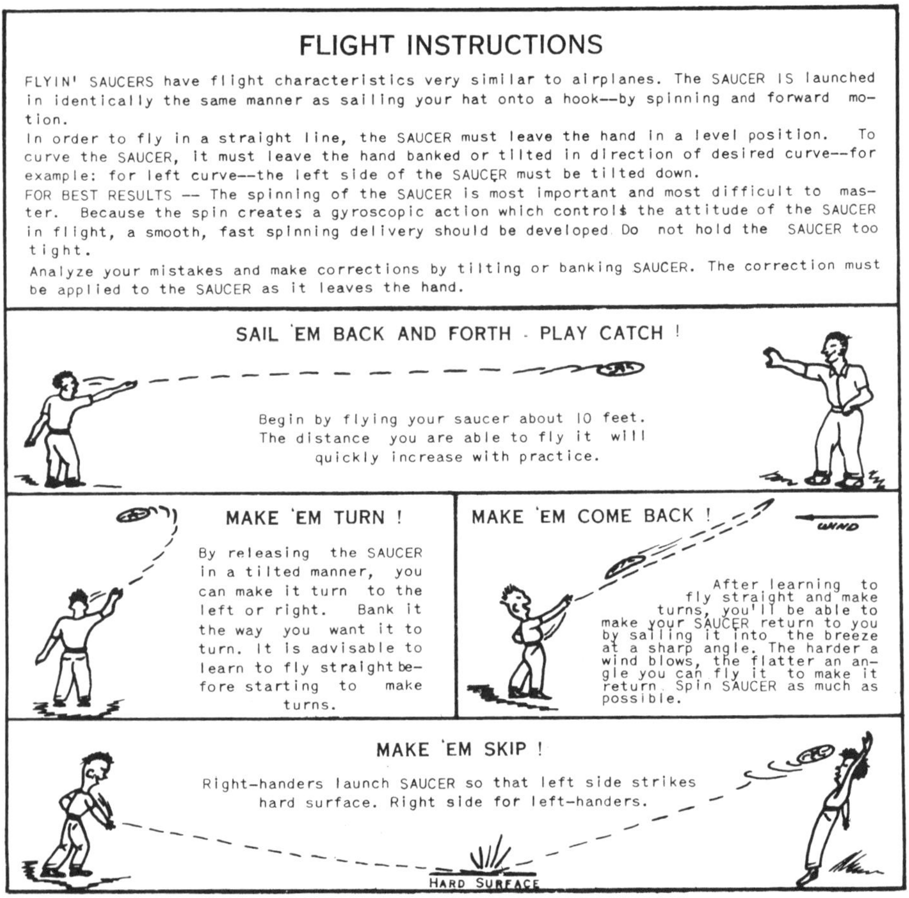

FLIGHT INSTRUCTIONS

FLYIN' SAUCERS have flight characteristics very similar to airplanes. The SAUCER IS launched in identically the same manner as sailing your hat onto a hook--by spinning and forward motion.

In order to fly in a straight line, the SAUCER must leave the hand in a level position. To curve the SAUCER, it must leave the hand banked or tilted in direction of desired curve--for example: for left curve--the left side of the SAUCER must be tilted down.

FOR BEST RESULTS -- The spinning of the SAUCER is most important and most difficult to master. Because the spin creates a gyroscopic action which controls the attitude of the SAUCER in flight, a smooth, fast spinning delivery should be developed. Do not hold the SAUCER too tight.

Analyze your mistakes and make corrections by tilting or banking SAUCER. The correction must be applied to the SAUCER as it leaves the hand.

SAIL 'EM BACK AND FORTH - PLAY CATCH !

Begin by flying your saucer about 10 feet. The distance you are able to fly it will quickly increase with practice.

MAKE 'EM TURN !

By releasing the SAUCER in a tilted manner, you can make it turn to the left or right. Bank it the way you want it to turn. It is advisable to learn to fly straight before starting to make turns.

MAKE 'EM COME BACK !

After learning to fly straight and make turns, you'll be able to make your SAUCER return to you by sailing it into the breeze at a sharp angle. The harder a wind blows, the flatter an angle you can fly it to make it return. Spin SAUCER as much as possible.

MAKE 'EM SKIP !

Right-handers launch SAUCER so that left side strikes hard surface. Right side for left-handers.

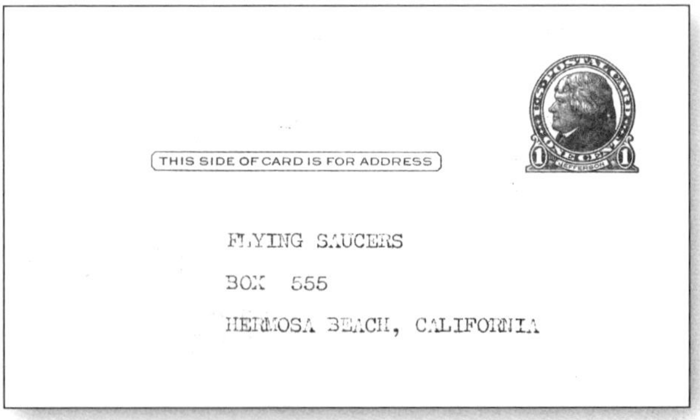

Flyin-Saucer reorder card—front side.

APPENDIX C—Game of Heckle: Pipco Flyin-Saucer—1949

THE GAME OF HECKLE

THE GAME OF HECKLE provides a means of utilizing the unique manner in which the FLYIN' SAUCER can be guided. Rules and regulations are provided, forming the basis for skill and competition

PLAYERS -- Four -- with two on each team.

OBJECT -- To fly SAUCER around HECKLERS into your partner's circle.

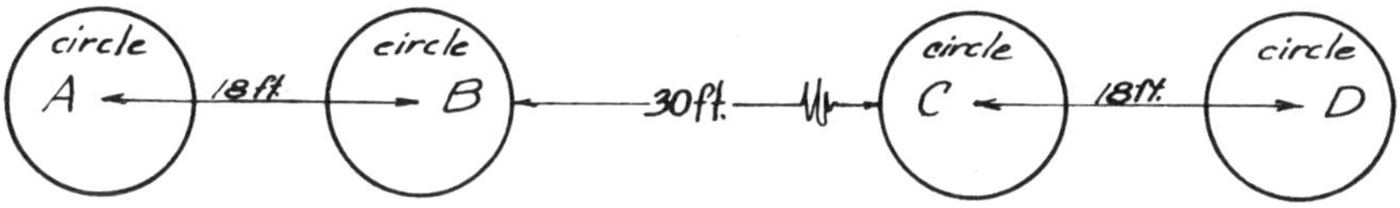

ALL CIRCLES ARE 6 FEET IN DIAMETER -- CENTER SPACE MAY VARY WITH ABILITY.

All players must remain in their circle until SAUCER is airborne.

The game begins with the Flier (A) attempting to sail the SAUCER around the HECKLERS in the circles (B) and (C) so that his partner in the Receiver's circle (D) can catch it.

Flier (A) must remain in his circle when serving the SAUCER.

HECKLER (B) must remain in his circle at all times while his team is defensive. He may attempt to stop the flight of the SAUCER, or distract the Flier in any manner. Should he step or fall out of his circle, his team forfeits 1 point and the offensive team retains serve.

HECKLER (C) remains in his circle until SAUCER is airborne. He may then leave his circle to heckle the Receiver (D) in any manner so long as he doesn't interfere with flight of SAUCER or touch the Receiver, or step into the Receiver's circle. Hecklers forfeit 2 points for each infraction.

Receiver (D) attempts to catch the SAUCER in his circle. Should he do so, then his team receives 2 points. Should it be necessary for the Receiver to leave his circle to catch the SAUCER, then his team scores but 1 point. Should he drop or miss the SAUCER, no points are scored, and the teams change positions. (A) changes with (B) and (C) changes with (D).

(C) is now the Flier, and (B) the Receiver. HECKLER (D) must remain in his circle, and the HECKLER (A) becomes the roving HECKLER.

Teams change positions when the Receiver fails to catch the SAUCER.

In the event that no Referee is available, disputes will be settled by mutual agreement, or the flip of a coin.

First team to score 25 points wins the game.

KEEP 'EM FLYIN'

This is a PIPCO PRODUCT — San Luis Obispo, Calif.

FLYING SAUCER ORDER BLANK

Please send me ____ more FLYING SAUCER(S)

Name______________________________

Address____________________________

City__________ Zone____ State__________

CHECK ONE ONLY:

☐ SHIP SAUCER(S) C.O.D. $1.00 each plus a few cents handling charges.

☐ OK, I will enclose this order in an envelope with $1.00 for each one ordered and Please SHIP PREPAID.

Flyin-Saucer reorder card—back side.

Poly bag with outrageous copy written by Fred Morrison

ENLISTMENT FORM

Being of sound mind and complete control of my finances, I would like to become a PLUTO PLATTER PILOT.

Name

Please Print

Address

City and State

Age Height Intestinal Fortitude Amount Devout Yes or No (if neither explain)

I would like a ☐ Red; ☐ Yellow; ☐ Green or ☐ White PLUTO PLATTER (S) as sanctioned by ADMIRAL ASTEROID, Conqueror of the Cosmic All.

All answers are true to the best of my knowledge and I enclose $1.10 for each PLUTO PLATTER and SPACE LICENSE.

Send to Space Headquarters

AMERICAN TRENDS CO.

15838 HARVEST MOON, LA PUENTE, CALIFORNIA

SEND THIS CARD We Will Mail Prepaid or C.O.D.

THIS IS YOUR ALL COSMIC IDENTIFICATION

Pluto Platter Space License

This CERTIFICATE bears valid testimonial that the undersigned is authorized to celestial navigate in any multi-stage PLUTO PLATTER space craft in all universes sanctioned by ADMIRAL ASTEROID.

The civil, military and cosmic authorities are respectfully requested to extend every courtesy to the holder of this space craft license.

Licensee Sign Here

Registered With
SPACE HEADQUARTERS
AMERICAN TRENDS CO., U.S.A.

Signed *Admiral Asteroid*
CONQUEROR OF THE COSMIC ALL

Reorder Card at top came with the very few American Trends Pluto Platters that were packaged. The Space License at the bottom was sent with reordered discs.

WHAM-O FLYING SAUCER GAME INSTRUCTIONS

Flying Saucer court is laid out as in diagram with the 2 posts set anywhere from about 20 feet up to 40 feet apart, depending on how large an area is available.

Game is played with 2 or more players. Saucers are thrown from one end of court towards the opposite post and then back. The object is to get the saucers close to the post, and, if possible, to hit it.

SCORING:

Closest saucer to post	-1 point
Saucer hitting post	-3 points
Farthest saucer from post	-minus 1 point

First man or team to make a total of 10 points wins game. Can be team play or individual scoring.

Rope attached to posts is for measuring closest or farthest saucers accurately.

COURT

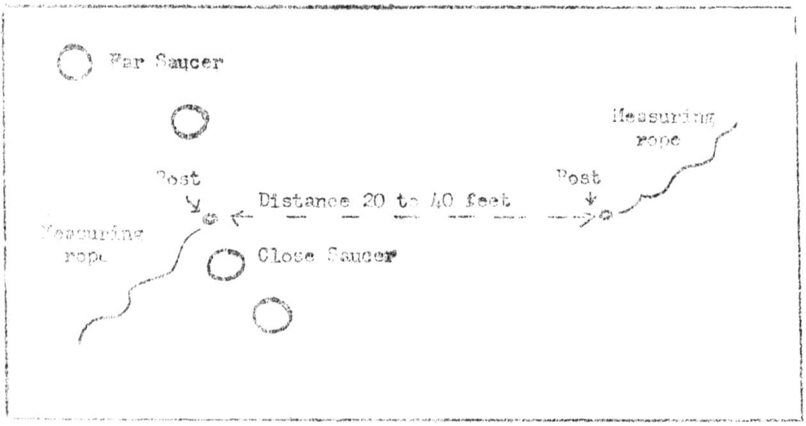

The earliest Wham-O Horseshoe Game sets from 1957 had two red and two white Pluto Platters with no measuring strings or instructions. The first instructions in 1958 were mimeograph copies, but were soon replaced with printed versions.

APPENDIX G—Zo-Lar Disc Insert with Instructions—1958

INSTRUCTIONS

FRISBEE CAN BE PLAYED WITH EITHER TWO PLAYERS, OR A GROUP OF PLAYERS, DIVIDED INTO TEAMS. ONLY TWO PLAYERS PLAY AT A TIME, EACH ONE IN LINE TAKING A TURN. THE PLAYERS SHOULD STAND ON A SPOT PLACED ABOUT 30 FT. APART. ONE FOOT MUST STAY ON THIS SPOT WHILE THE OTHER FOOT IS ALLOWED TO MOVE AROUND FREELY. A COIN MAY BE TOSSED TO SEE WHICH SIDE GOES FIRST.

THE OBJECT OF THE GAME IS TO GLIDE THE SAUCER WITHIN REACH OF YOUR OPPONENT. IF HE FAILS TO CATCH IT, OR MOVES HIS FOOT OFF THE SPOT, IT COUNTS AS A POINT FOR YOU. IF HE TOUCHES THE SAUCER, BUT FAILS TO CATCH IT, THIS ALSO COUNTS AS A POINT FOR YOU. IF YOUR OPPONENT CATCHES THE SAUCER WITH ONE HAND (EITHER HAND, BUT ONLY ONE HAND CAN BE USED), HE RECEIVES A POINT. IF YOU SAIL IT OUT OF HIS REACH, HE RECEIVES A POINT. NOW IT'S YOUR OPPONENT'S TURN TO TRY AND SCORE A POINT BY GLIDING THE SAUCER TO YOU.

THE FIRST TEAM TO SCORE 21 POINTS WINS.

EMPIRE PLASTIC, PELHAM MANOR, N. Y. NO.

United States Patent Office

Des. 183,626
Patented Sept. 30, 1958

183,626

FLYING TOY

Walter Frederick Morrison, La Puente, Calif.

Application July 22, 1957, Serial No. 47,035

Term of patent 7 years

(Cl. D34—15)

FIG. 1.

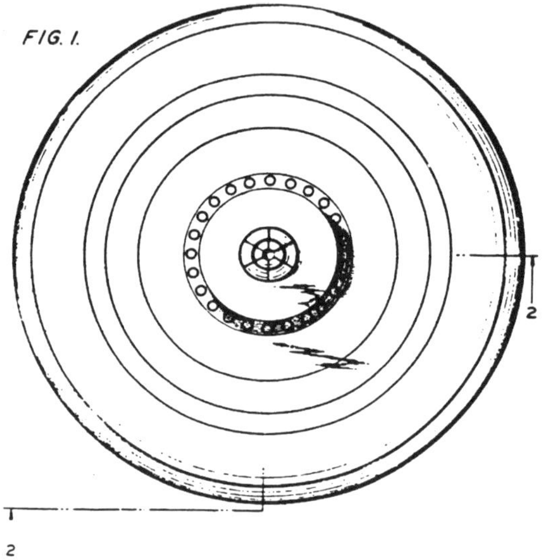

FIG. 2.

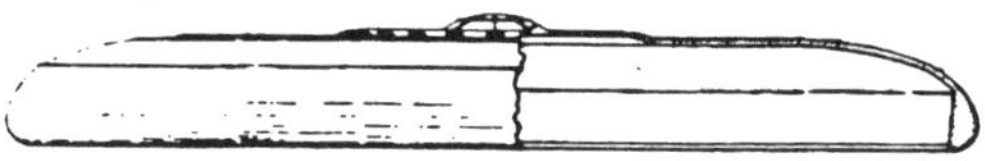

Fig. 1 is a top plan view of a flying toy, showing my new design;

Fig. 2 is a side elevational view thereof, partly in cross section taken on line **2—2** in Fig. 1.

I claim:

The ornamental design for a flying toy, as shown.

References Cited in the file of this patent

UNITED STATES PATENTS

D. 137,521	Davidson	Mar. 28, 1944
1,404,132	Manes	Jan. 17, 1922
2,690,339	Hall	Sept. 28, 1954

FOREIGN PATENTS

890,001	France	Oct. 25, 1943

INSTRUCTIONS FOR PLAYING

SKY CROQUET

...the streamlined space-age way to play croquet, ...and SKY GOLF, too!

. . . PLAY CROQUET

SET PARALLEL

SET OBLIQUE

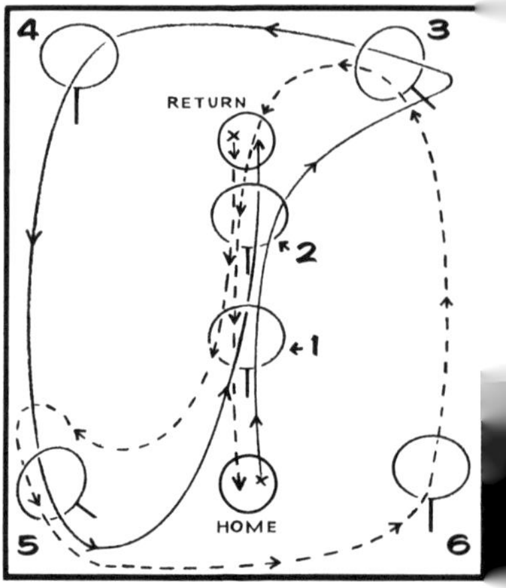

——→ = OUTWARD TRIP = 1-2-3-4-5-1-2

– – –→ = RETURN TRIP = 2-1-5-6-3-2-1

In SKY CROQUET 2 to 6 players use SKY SAUCERS instead of mallets and balls . . . SPACE STATIONS in place of wickets and LAUNCHING PADS rather than stakes.

Any convenient, playing area (UNIVERSE) is selected, the 6 SPACE STATIONS are assembled (by joining the hoop part to the fork part) and pushed into the ground at points shown in DIAGRAM . . . and the "HOME" and "RETURN" LAUNCHING PADS (the 2 red rings) are placed in the positions shown. A suggested distance between launching pads and space stations (1) and (2) is four feet . . . also between these two space stations. And a suggested distance between space stations (3) (4) (5) and (6) is 25 to 40 feet . . . or any size square or rectangle to fit your playing area.

SPACE STATIONS

#1 = Earth	#3 = Jupiter	#5 = Mercury
#2 = Mars	#4 = Saturn	#6 = Venus

SKY SAUCER COLORS

RED = First	BLUE = Third	GREEN = Fifth
WHITE = Second	YELLOW = Fourth	ORANGE = Sixth

OBJECT OF THE GAME

Each player in order takes turns launching his sky saucer from the Home Launching Pad (and later from the Return Launching Pad) and gets refueled (earns another shot) each time he sails his saucer through a Space Station in the proper direction (See diagram).

The FIRST PLAYER to bring his saucer to rest INSIDE the Home Launching Pad wins the game.

HOW TO PLAY

Sail your Saucer level to make it go straight . . . tip to right, to go right . . . tip to left, to go left. Use wrist motion.

- First Player (with one foot in the Home Launching Pad) sails his Saucer through Space Station #1 and gets another shot to try through #2, and if successful earns another shot to go for #3.
- If on his take-off, he travels through both #1 and #2, he gets two more shots to try to pass through #3.
- In other words, each station through which a player passes in the proper direction earns him another shot.

E MODERN WAY . . .

UE

LEL

A player always stands on his saucer's landing spot, when making his next shot.

- At the half-way point, a player completes his Outward Trip by landing his saucer inside the Return Launching Pad, which earns him one shot to take off for his return trip (with one foot in launching pad, as before).

- When a player miscalculates his course of flight and fails to launch his saucer so as to pass through the proper station in the proper direction, he is grounded and does not have any more shots till all the following players (in order) have likewise become grounded.

- Any saucer landing outside the UNIVERSE is immediately placed just inside the nearest edge of the playing area.

ORBITING

- If a player's saucer touches any other player's saucer in landing, the player gets two shots OR he may ORBIT (sail his opponent's saucer anywhere inside the playing area – UNIVERSE – to get the opponent off course) ... and then use the remaining one shot for his own saucer's flight.

- If the Orbiting Player miscalculates and ORBITS his opponent's saucer outside the Universe, he forfeits the second shot he would otherwise have received. In addition, the opponent immediately ORBITS the saucer of the first Orbiting Player.

- Any saucers orbited outside the Universe are promptly returned to a point just inside the nearest edge of the playing area.

- A player cannot gain extra shots or orbit the same player again until he has passed through his next space station or landed in the Return Launching Pad at the halfway point in his flight.

PLAYING PARTNERS

- Teams of two players each may compete in Sky Croquet.

- Play is similar to individual play, except partners may assist each other by HELPFUL ORBITING (sailing the partner's saucer to a better position and putting him back on course) . . . or by UNFAVORABLY ORBITING an opponent's saucer (sailing him off course or into a position where the partner can also orbit the same opponent . . . or gain two shots).

- Both partners must complete the game to win. Partners never follow each other (an opposing player must intervene with his turn).

- A player whose saucer has passed through all space stations and has only to land inside the Home Launching Pad to finish the game may become a FREE SATELLITE. By not landing inside the Home Launching Pad, such player may continue playing to aid his partner and orbit opponents off course.

Play SKY GOLF too!

Sail your Saucer level to make it go straight . . . tip to right, to go right . . . tip to left, to go left. Use wrist motion.

- The equipment of Sky Croquet may also be used to play SKY GOLF.
- The 6 space stations are located in any manner desired to make a six-hole miniature "golf course."
- The object of the game is to pass through each space station (hole out) by making as few shots as possible.
- One of the launching pads may be used for the first tee. For all the other tees, the player merely stands to the right of the space station (hole) just completed, when teeing off.
- There is no orbiting in Sky Golf. Any number up to six may play. Order of play is the same as in Sky Croquet (See Saucer Color Order of Play).
- All players complete each hole (pass through space station) and mark their scores . . . before play proceeds to the next hole.
- There is a penalty of one stroke for going out of bounds on a shot (out of the playing area or UNIVERSE). Out-of-bound shots are returned just inside bounds at nearest point.
- Par for each space station (hole) is determined and agreed upon, based on distance of hole and obstacles involved. Par for the course is the total of the pars for the six holes.
- In laying out the course and locating the space stations, shrubbery, trees or any other objects may be used as hazards or traps to add interest to the play. No limitation exists as to size of the layout. It can be made to fit your grounds.

SKY CROQUET and SKY GOLF are Products of--

COPAR...CHICAGO

APPENDIX J—Bob Healy to Ed Headrick Letter—1967

Investors DIVERSIFIED SERVICES, INC.

C O P Y

April 7, 1967

Mr. Edward E. Headrick
The Man from Wham-o
Wham-o Manufacturing Co.
835 E. El Monte Street
San Gabriel, California 91778

Dear Ed:

I enjoyed talking with you yesterday. It's nice to find someone who has a real appreciation of frisbee. You know, there is a certain spirit, an elan, an outlook, that separates a frisbee lover from ordinary folk and even though you're somewhat limited as a player I believe you have the spirit. It must result from spending so much time in the frisbee stamping plant.

As I mentioned, our director, Harvey J. Kuckuk, is interested in advancing the sport of frisbee, combing the country and the world to find the best possible competition, and finding out whether Ed Headrich, self-designated Father of Frisbee, can handle himself in a Guts Frisbee match.

Mr. Kuckuk can't understand why the Father of Frisbee has been unable to attend any of the first nine International Frisbee Tournaments. I've explained that you probably were busy at the frisbee stamping plant (or perhaps licking labels) on those days and couldn't see your way clear to make the Tournaments. Mr. Kuckuk then wonders why, if he doesn't attend the Tournaments, the Father of Frisbee claims to be the champion frisbee player. Frankly, on that point, I can offer nothing in your defense. I will say that I don't believe the reports that your appearance on the Tonight Show with the sixteen pound Superball led people to believe you are devious and unsavory. Some people, through no fault of theirs (remember Nixon?) don't come through on TV, and I think Mr. Kuckuk was unfair to base his judgement on a ten-minute secondhand acquaintanceship. I mention all this only to let you know that our able, industrious, and highly revered director who is devoting his life to the advancement of frisbee has serious doubts about the existence of the Father of the Frisbee. You can imagine the implications of such thoughts. Does Ford Frick go to bed wondering whether Abner Doubleday really paced off that diamond in the cow pasture? Did Maurice Podoloff seriously doubt that Dr. Naismith knew what he was doing

See page 68 for the full story about this letter.

Mr. Edward E. Headrick -2- April 7, 1967

when he nailed the peach basket to the wall? Harvey Kuckuk is so uncertain that he sometimes turns Ed Headrick's picture to the wall. At times he is not even sure it is Ed Headrick's picture.

But enough of Harvey's troubles. The Tournament this year will be held on July 2nd, same place, same time (Eagle Harbor Ballyard, Eagle Harbor, Michigan). We've been thinking of using bumper stickers to promote the Tournament and wonder whether your art department can come up with a suitable rendering of a frisbee in flight, or perhaps of a hand about to release a frisbee.

I'm enclosing some material relating to last year's Tournament. Of particular interest to you should be our architects description of the International Frisbee Pavilion. This project hasn't moved as rapidly as we hoped because of the tight mortgage money situation but we're sticking to our original goals.

Yours for better frisbee,

Robert H. Healy

RHH:pam

APPENDIX K—Wham-O IFA Application Form—1967

©1967 **INTERNATIONAL FRISBEE® ASSOCIATION**

2900 Rowena Avenue
Los Angeles, California 90039

I would like to become a member of the International Frisbee® Association. Please send me my official IFA membership card, IFA membership certificate, FRISBEE® manual, proficiency qualification form and the FRISBEE® Newsletter as fast as you can. I have enclosed a 50¢ membership fee (no stamps, please), which qualifies me as a FRISBEE® Novice and which also covers handling and mailing costs.

NAME______________________________ AGE______ SEX______
(Please Print)

ADDRESS______________________________
(Number) (Street)

____
(City) (State) (Zip)

Which model FRISBEE® do you own?

REGULAR___ PROFESSIONAL___ MASTER TOURNAMENT___ MINI-FRISBEE®___

The proficiency qualification form will give you the requirements necessary to establish your individual classification under IFA world-wide standards — Amateur, Expert, or Master.

INSERT 50¢ MEMBERSHIP FEE
PLACE IN ENVELOPE and MAIL

PLACE COIN HERE

PLACE COIN HERE

TO: INTERNATIONAL FRISBEE® ASSN.
2900 Rowena Ave, Los Angeles, Calif. 90039

©1967 **INTERNATIONAL FRISBEE® ASSOCIATION**

2900 Rowena Avenue
Los Angeles, California 90039

Dec. 26, 1967 E. E. HEADRICK **3,359,678**

FLYING SAUCER

Filed Nov. 1, 1965 2 Sheets-Sheet 1

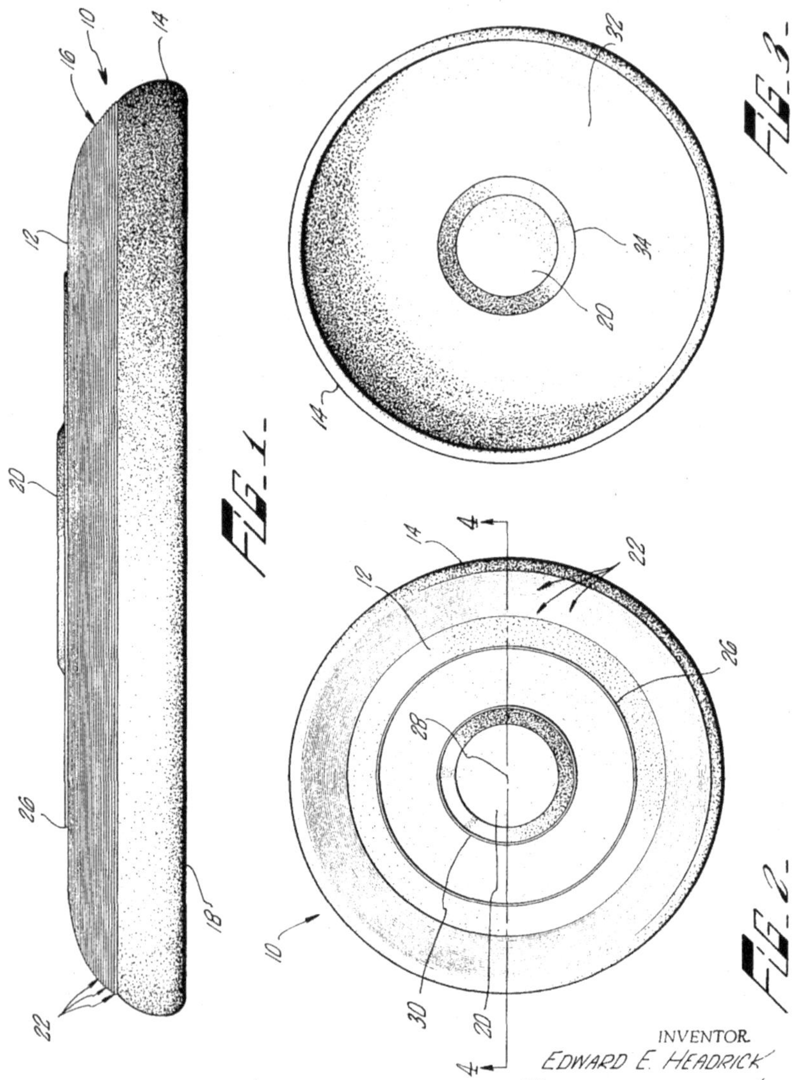

INVENTOR
EDWARD E. HEADRICK
BY
Christie, Parker & Hale
ATTORNEYS

APPENDIX M—Fling-n-Ring Instructions— c. 1970

NEW!

FLiNG-n-RiNG

TM

PAT. PEND.

TOURNAMENTS   FAMILY FUN   8 CAN PLAY

Young and old alike will go for this versatile, safe, fun-filled new game — great sport for one, two, four or eight players (in two sets of four, using one peg per set of flingers).

TOSS AND SCORE LIKE HORSESHOES — GAME IS 21 POINTS

Little ringer (any small hole)	scores 5 points
Ringer (large center hole)	scores 3 points
Leaner	scores 2 points
Closest to peg	scores 1 point

INVENT YOUR OWN VARIATIONS

Example: Player tosses flinger and opponent attempts to ring it by moving peg into receiving position.

Fling-n-Ring SET INCLUDES: 4 flingers, 2 pegs

Safe . . . . weatherproof . . . . almost indestructible with normal use.

* DEALER INQUIRIES INVITED

NEWHART PRODUCTS, INC.
Milford, Connecticut 06460

APPENDIX N—Frisbee World Magazine, Issue 1: Feb. 1976

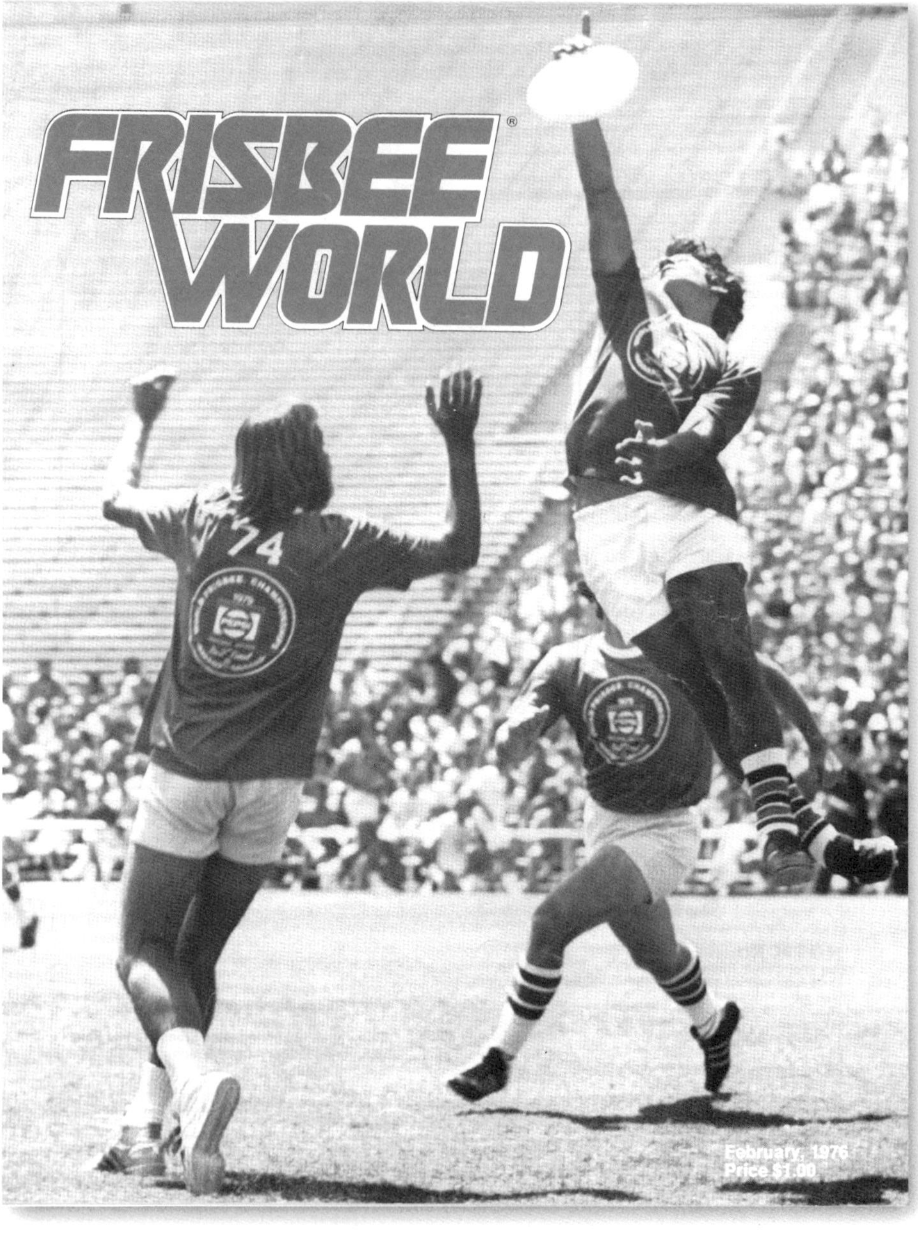

APPENDIX O—Disc Golf Object Course—1976

HOLE	YDS	PAR	GOAL
1	85	3	Telephone pole
2	53	2	Telephone pole
3	135	4	Drinking fountain
4	160	5	Drinking fountain
5	120	4	Tree in clearing (past row of trees)
6	155	4	Trunk of large tree at edge of bushes
7	155	4	Trunk of small tree next to road
8	100	3	Trunk of large tree at bottom of hill
9	180	5	Trunk of large tree with light bark, in middle of clearing
	1143	34	TOTAL OUT
10	60	2	Trunk of tree at edge of clearing
11	100	3	Trunk of large tree
12	130	4	Trunk of pine tree in middle of clearing
13	110	4	Trunk of tree at corner of clearing
14	50	2	Trash barrel
15	115	4	Trunk of tree at fork of path
16	95	3	Trunk of tree to left of small clearing
17	135	4	Drinking fountain
18	230	6	Trunk of large tree near road
	1025	32	TOTAL IN
	2168	66	TOTAL COURSE

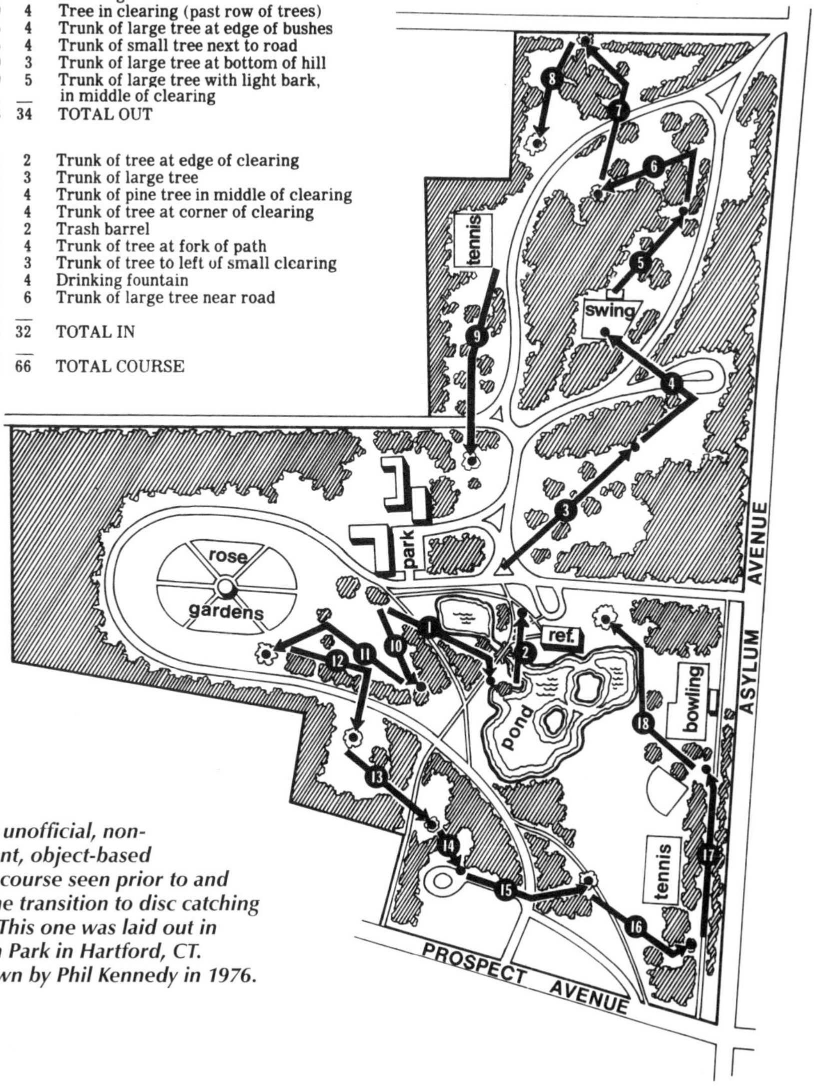

A typical unofficial, non-permanent, object-based disc golf course seen prior to and during the transition to disc catching devices. This one was laid out in Elizabeth Park in Hartford, CT. Map drawn by Phil Kennedy in 1976.

APPENDIX P—Oak Grove Tee Sign & Score card

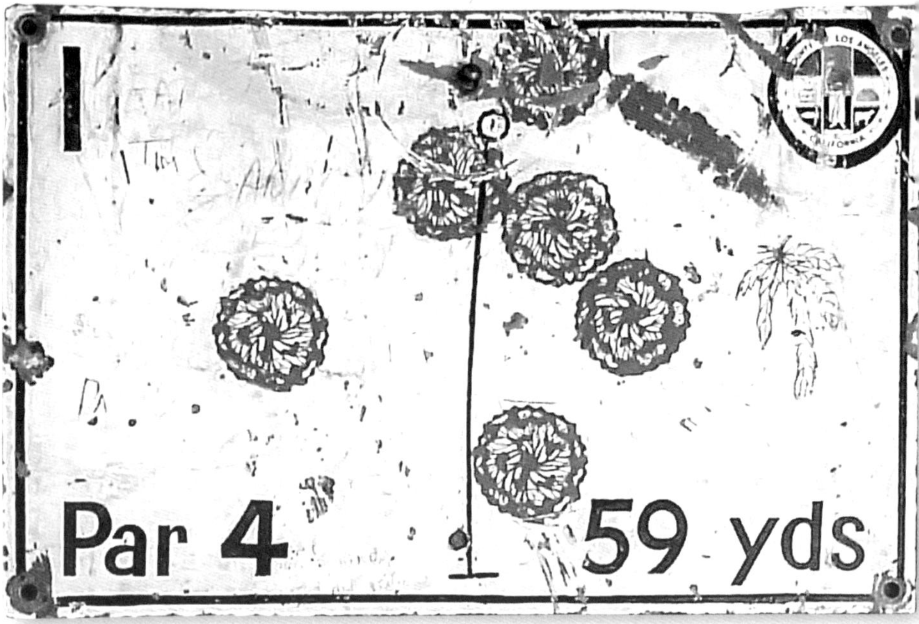

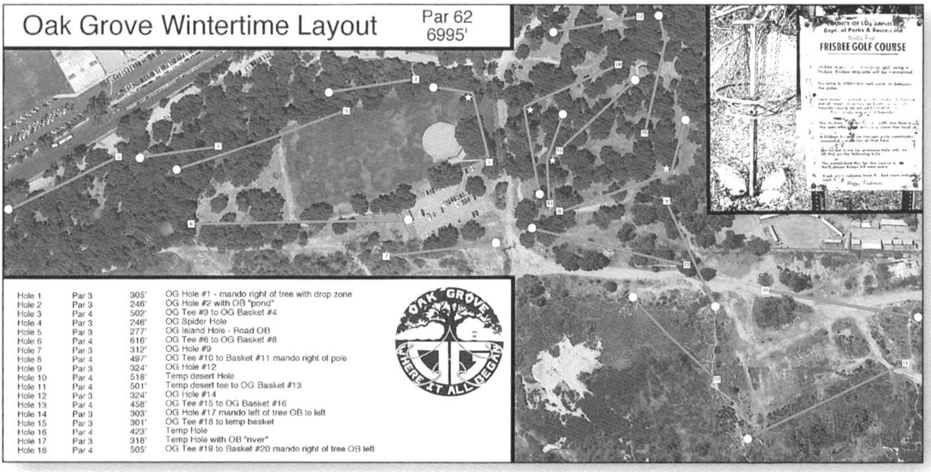

At top is the tee sign for hole one of the original Oak Grove Disc Golf Course in La Cañada, CA (the very first DGA chained Pole Hole course) designed by Ed Headrick. (See full story beginning on page 135.) At bottom is a modern score card from the course.

A Colorful Collection of Tins, Lids, and Flying Saucers from The Early Days of Disc Golf

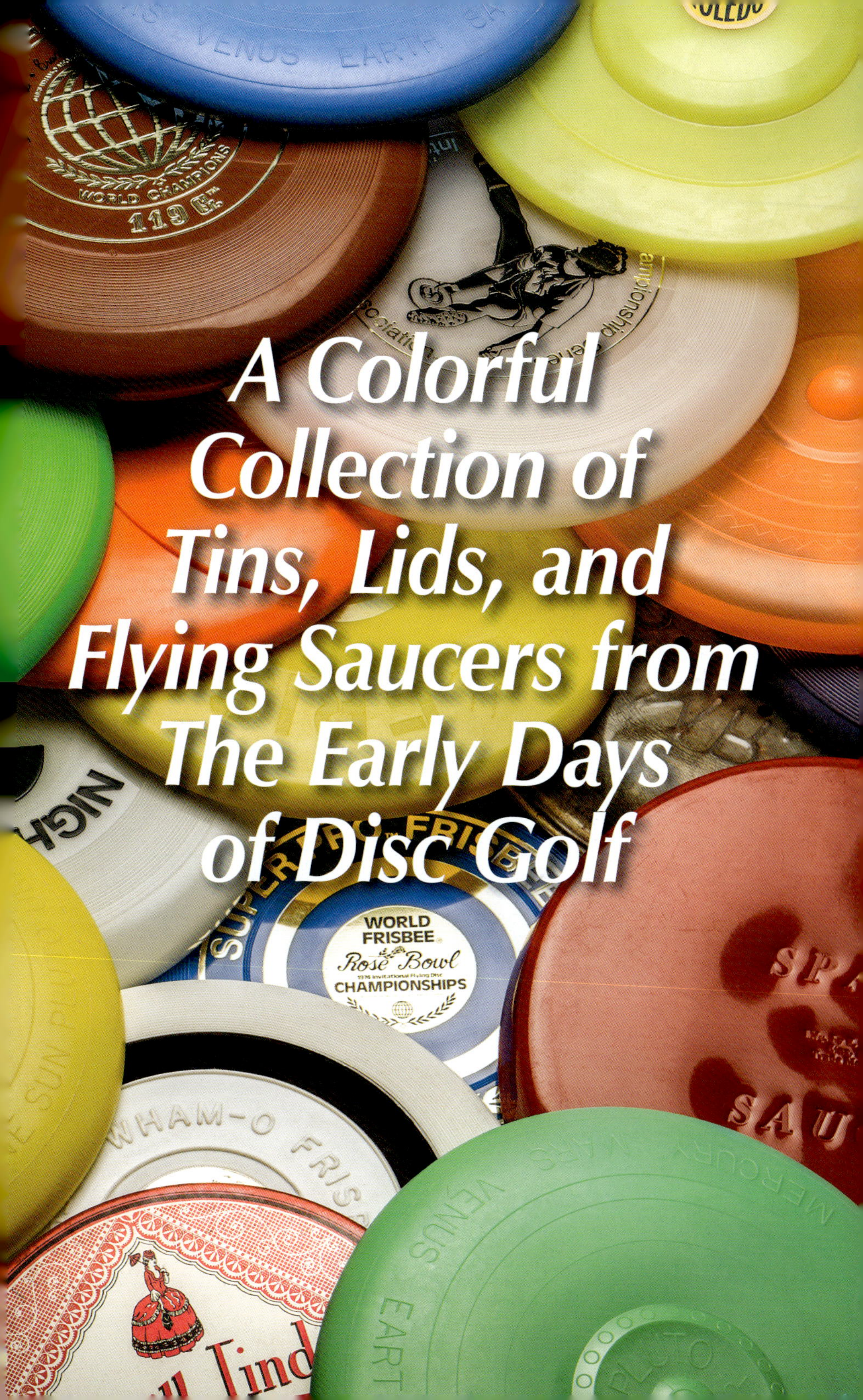

Flyable Container Lids & Pie Tins

The Flyin-Saucer & Its Evolution

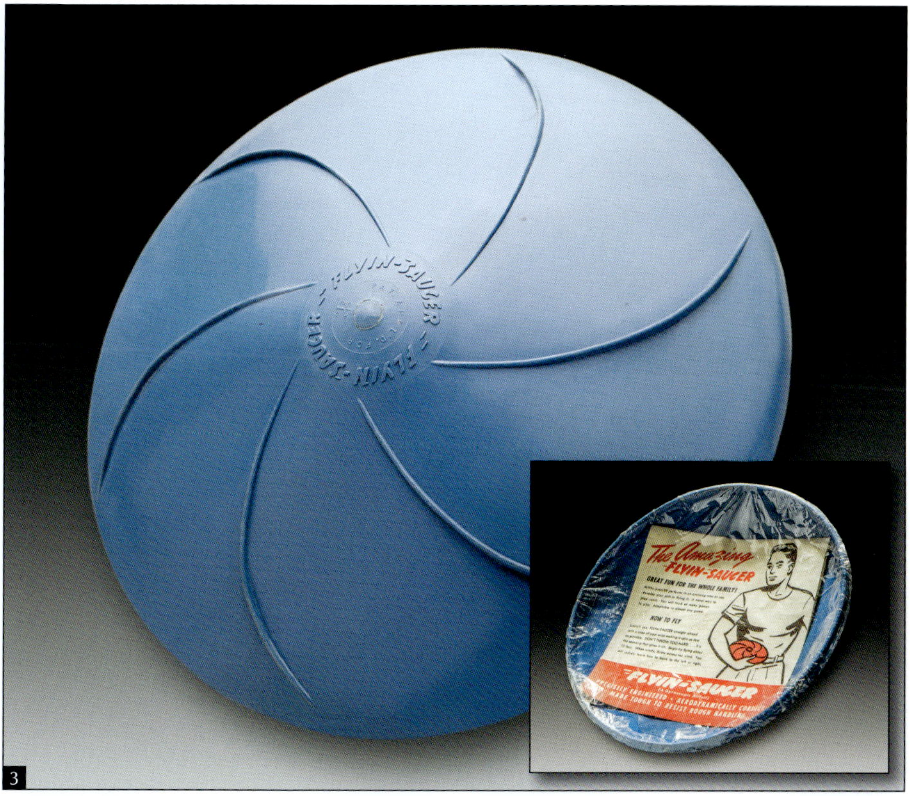

3

4

5

1—Flyable container lids, covers, cake pans, mats, etc. of the type tossed before plastic discs.

2—Pie tins from bakeries all over the world were likely tossed.

3—Fred Morrison-designed Flyin-Saucer is the earliest known plastic flying disc. (1948–50)

4—In 1953 Southern California Plastic began making Flyin Saucers from flexible polyethylene plastic. One was given to Dan "Stork" Roddick in 1953. (See page 132.)

5—By the 1980s the original Flyin-Saucer mold had been modified at least 13 times!

The Space Saucer & Its Evolution

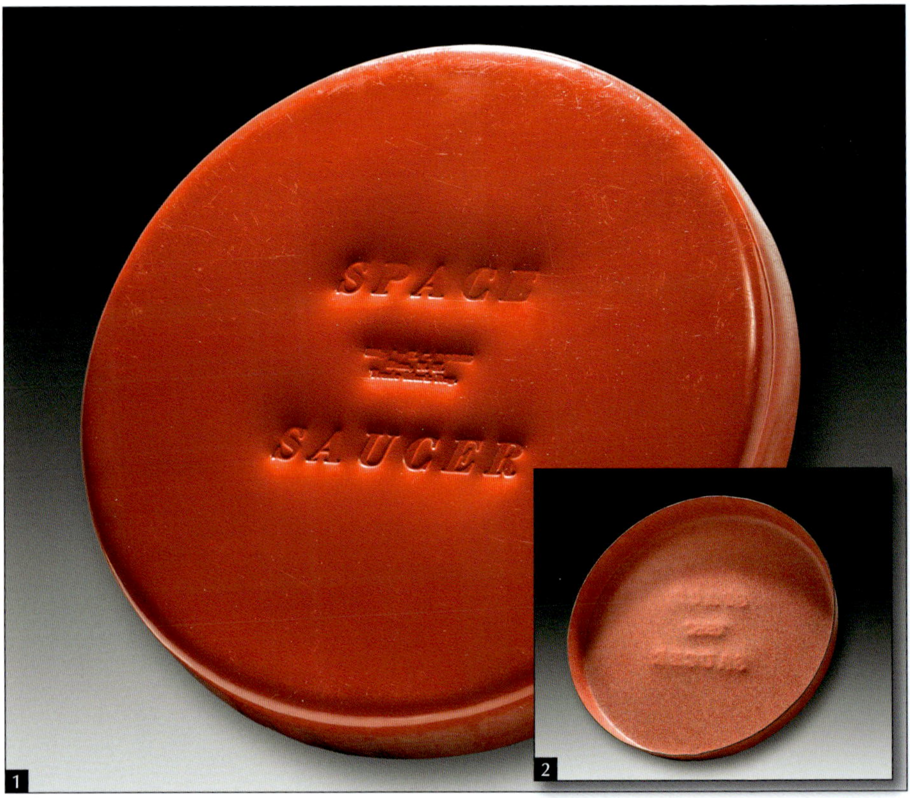

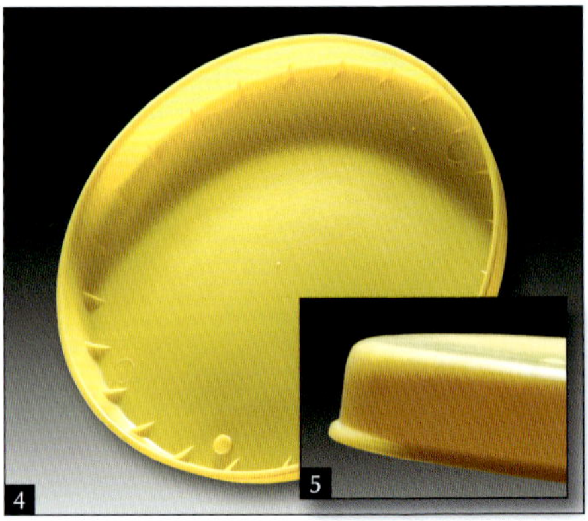

1—Space Saucer prototypes were made from flat sheets of hot Boltaron plastic pressed into a lid-shaped form, then hand trimmed. (1953–54)

2—Early Space Saucers have no thickened rims.

3—1955–60 Space Saucers were injection molded.

4—1955–60 Space Saucers have various configurations of corner buttresses underneath to reinforce the thin rims.

5—1959–60 Space Saucers have slightly thicker rims and the word "Frisbee" on the package.

The Pluto Platter & Its Evolution

1

THIS IS YOUR ALL COSMIC IDENTIFICATION

Pluto Platter Space License

This CERTIFICATE bears valid testimonial that the undersigned is authorized to celestial navigate in any multi-stage PLUTO PLATTER space craft in all universes sanctioned by ADMIRAL ASTEROID.

The civil, military and cosmic authorities are respectfully requested to extend every courtesy to the holder of this space craft license.

Licensee Sign Here.

Registered With
SPACE HEADQUARTERS
AMERICAN TRENDS CO., U.S.A.

Signed *Admiral Asteroid*
CONQUEROR OF THE COSMIC ALL

2

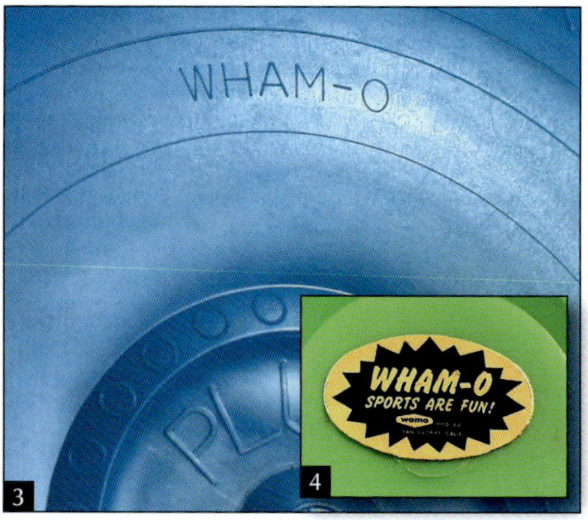

3

4

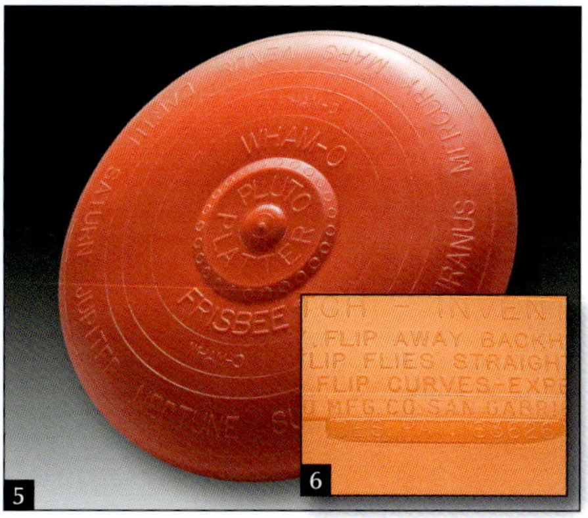

5

6

1—American Trends Pluto Platter designed & marketed by Fred Morrison. (1955–1957)

2—Pluto Platter Space Licenses were issued to folks who filled out a return card.

3—1957 Wham-O Pluto Platters have only one small "Wham-O" name added to the top side.

4—1957 Pluto Platters have a sticker underneath.

5—1958–1964 Pluto Platters came in six mold variations; all with "Frisbee" and a large "Wham-O" on the top.

6—Changes were made by routing out the old text creating raised bars or "eskers."

Horseshoe & Frisbee Jr. Sets

1

2

3

4

5

1—1957-58 Horseshoe sets still had older "wamo" name on the box w/ 2, later 3-color paper labels.

2—1957 Sets have only white & red discs, and no measuring strings or instructions.

3—1958 Sets have a mix of disc colors, strings, & instructions (mimeographed, later printed).

4—1967–72 Sets come in a variety of packaging and contents; discs include Flying Saucers, Horseshoe Models, & Regular Models.

5—Frisbee Jr. set from Transgram has 4 mini-sized discs. Header card has instructions for a "golf" game using posts or trees as targets. (1958) Photo by Marvin Paul.

Sky Croquet, Fling-n-Ring, & Ring Fling Sets

1

2

4

3

1—Sky Croquet set from Copar has 6 Sky Saucers & wire hoops as targets. Also has instructions for playing "Sky Golf." (1960-62)

2—Fling-n-Ring set from Newhart Products has 4 discs & 2 stakes, boxed w/ instructions. (c.1970)

3—Ring Fling set from Kent has 2 hard, thin plastic saucers, metal poles, plastic hoops, & connector straps. (Early-1970s)

4—Ring Fling set from Eagle has better quality components & instructions. (Mid-1970s)

Variations on the Pluto Platter Design

1

2

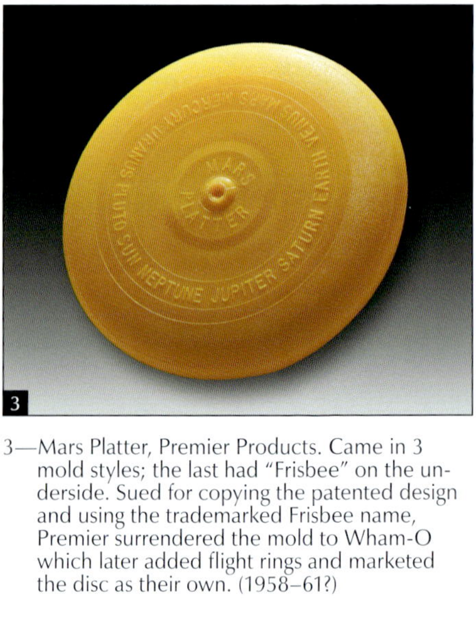

3

1—Wham-O Flying Saucer. Slightly smaller than the Pluto Platter. Came w/ & w/o planet names in several mold variations & colors; late versions have flight rings. (1958–66)

2—Sailing Satellite. 1st Wham-O created disc. Silver ('57) & colors ('58). Dropped for its too large size & Hula Hoop craze production. (1957–58)

3—Mars Platter, Premier Products. Came in 3 mold styles; the last had "Frisbee" on the underside. Sued for copying the patented design and using the trademarked Frisbee name, Premier surrendered the mold to Wham-O which later added flight rings and marketed the disc as their own. (1958–61?)

Discs of the Late-1950s & Early-1960s

1

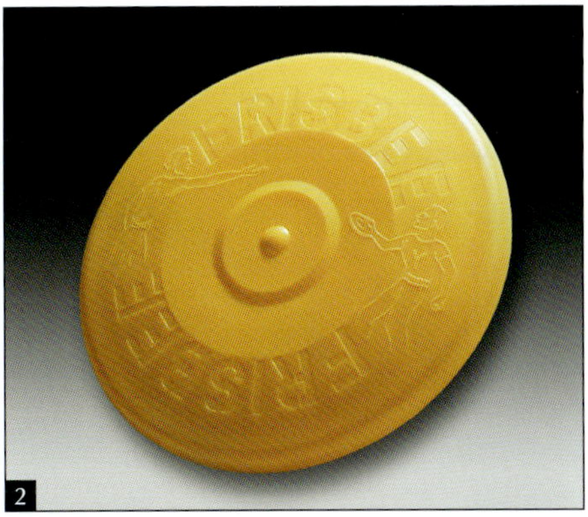
2

3

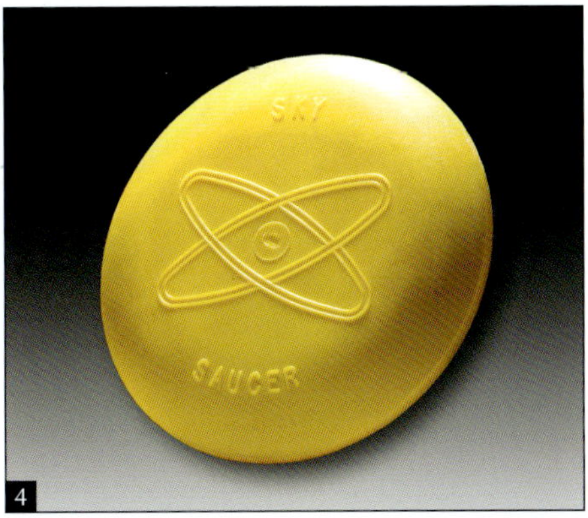

4

5

6

1—Zo-Lar, Empire Plastics. Packaging says "Play Frisbee." (1958)

2—"Mystery Y," Empire Plastics was made from a retooled Zo-Lar mold. Box has "Frisbee" on it. (1959–1961?)

3—Jumping Jupiter, Irwin Corp. (late 1950s)

4—Sky Saucer, Copar. 6 Came in Sky Croquet sets. Also packaged singly & 2-disc sets. (1960–62)

5— Twirl-A-Boom, mfr. unknown. (Early 1960s)

6— Holy Toledo, Auburn Rubber. (1964)

The Evolution From "Toy" Saucers to "Sport" Discs

1

1—The Official Pro Model, Wham-O. In early fall of 1964 Ed Headrick had the Pluto Platter mold retooled to create a brand new look to capture the burgeoning sports market. Gone were the toy-like, space-oriented features…in was a sexy broad racing stripe, a thicker rim for increased stability, and a series of flight rings. (These ridges were claimed to increase air turbulence and add stability. No test documents have been published to support these claims, but a full patent was nevertheless awarded in 1967.) The band was spray painted on the 1st & 2nd versions, and screened on later versions. The Olympic Rings logo was used on the label until the Olympic Committee objected. It was replaced with a Wham-O Frisbee design. The Pro has gone through numerous iterations over the years and is still currently available. Extending the importance of the legendary Pluto Platter, the Pro is undoubtedly one of the most influential early Disc Golf era discs. (1964–present)

2

2—Regular Model, Wham-O. Retooled Flying Saucer mold. Probably the most ubiquitous disc ever made! (1966–present)

Discs of the Late-1960s

1

2

3

4

5

6

1—Horseshoe Model, Wham-O. Retooled "Junior Flying Saucer" (1958) & "Speedy." (1966)

2—Flying Saucer, Remco. (Late-1960s)

3—Master Tournament Model, Wham-O. Originally came boxed w/IFA application & registration papers. 1st official Ultimate disc. (1967–80s)

4—Flying Saucer, Whiffle. (1970s)

5—Moonlighter Frisbee, Wham-O. Pro mold variation. (1970s)

6—All-American Frisbee, Wham-O. Pro mold variation (1970s)

Discs of the Early to Mid-1970s

1—Fastback Frisbee, Wham-O. Original domed, multi-ringed design. (Early 1970s)

2—All Star, CPI. Was the golf disc of choice until Wham-O introduced the World Class discs. (Early 1970s)

3— Super Zinger, Chemtoy. (Mid-1970s)

4—One of many knock-offs, unknown. (Mid-1970s)

5—Tosserino, Aviva. (1970s)

6—Prototype 151G, Wham-O. w/Super Pro label & hotstamp. Excellent early golf disc. (Mid 1970s)

The Rise of Tournament Discs

1

2

3

4

5

6

1—WFC Pro, Wham-O. 1974 Rose Bowl label.

2—For PR value Wham-O invited Hollywood stars to many events. Michael Douglas & Karl Malden autographed Victor Malefronte's 1974 Rose Bowl Tournament Pro. "Not For Resale" label.

3— WFC Super Pro, Wham-O. 1974 Rose Bowl.

4—WFC Super Pro, Wham-O. 1974 Rose Bowl special label on underside

5—WFC Fastback, Wham-O. 1974 Rose Bowl.

6—1975 Octad Super Pro. Photo by Dan Roddick.

Tournament Discs Go Mass Market

1—IFT Pro, Wham-O. (1975)

2—1975 Rose Bowl WFC 119G & 151G versions, Wham-O.

3— The World Class Frisbee Series, Wham-O. Heavily marketed to the general public beginning in 1976, the WCF discs introduced many to the increasing emphasis Wham-O placed on supporting organized disc sports. From 1976 to 1982 the WFC series discs were available in an assortment of colors, hotstamps, & disc molds including 119G, 141G, 165G, & 97G. They also have become great collectors' items.

NAS: The Beginning of Open Tournaments

1—National Championship Series, Wham-O. Beginning in 1976 these discs were available in 4 standard colors (rare 1976 black "Jimmy" shown), as 119G & 141G versions, plus 165G after 1978. Available at NAS tournaments and through the IFA. Highly collectable.

2—National Championship Series, Wham-O. Special first run edition, 3 color hotstamp. (1976)

3—1976 WFC Rose Bowl 119G, Wham-O.

The Birth of True Golf Discs

1—Night Flyer, DGA. The first disc produced & marketed specifically for Disc Golf. 40 mold Wham-O discs using glow plastic for extra weight. Hotstamps #1–8 indicated increasing weights. The name was contested as trademarked forcing the DGA to rename the discs "Midnight Flyer" which were also produced from 50 & 51 molds.

2—Around Nine, DGA. Wham-O 40 mold. (1976)

3—Wham-O Fastback promoting the first PDGA tournament in New England. (1978)

Bibliography

BOOKS & CHAPTERS IN GENERAL WORKS

Caney, Steven. "The Invention of the Frisbee." In Steven Caney's *Invention Book,* pages 97–102. New York, NY: Workman Publishing Co., Inc., 1999.

Danna, Mark and Dan Poynter. *Frisbee Players Handbook.* Parachuting Publications, 1978.

Dickson, Paul. *The Mature Person's Guide to Kites, Yo Yos, Frisbees and Other Childlike Diversions,* pages 116–131. The New American Library. Plume Books, 1977.

Horowitz, Judy and Billy Bloom. *Frisbee, More Than Just a Game of Catch.* Champagne, IL: Leisure Press, 1983.

Johnson, Stancil, E.D. *FRISBEE: A Practitioner's Manual and Definitive Treatise.* New York, NY: Workman Publishing Co., Inc., 1975.

Malafronte, Victor A. *The Complete Book of Frisbee: The History of the Sport & The First Official Price Guide.* Alameda, CA: American Trends Publishing Co., 1998.

Morrison, Fred and Kennedy, Phil. *Flat Flip Flies Straight: True Origins of the Frisbee.* Wethersfield, CT: Wormhole Publishers, 2006.

New Frisbee—The New Games Book, pages 28–29. New York, NY: Doubleday & Co. Inc., A Headlands Press Book, 1976.

Norton, Goldy. *The Official Frisbee Handbook.* New York, NY: Bantam Books, 1972.

Olney, Ross R. *Tricky Discs: Frisbee Saucer Flying.* New York, NY: Lothrop, Lee & Shepard Company div., William Morrow & Co., 1979.

Panati, Charles. "Frisbee: Pre-1957, Connecticut." in *Extraordinary Origins of Everyday Things,* pages 372–373. New York, NY: Harper & Row, 1987.

Roddick, Dan. *Frisbee Disc Basics.* Englewood Cliffs, NJ: Prentice-Hall, 1980.

Roddick, Dan. *The Discourse.* San Gabriel, CA: Wham-O, Inc., 1978, 1986, 1989

Tips, Charles. *Frisbee by the Masters.* Millbrae, CA: Celestial Arts, 1977.

Tips, Charles and Dan Roddick. *Frisbee Sports & Games.* Millbrae, CA: Celestial Arts, 1979.

Wallechinsky, David and Irving Wallace. "Tossing The Discus." In *The People's Almanac #2,* page 1091. New York, NY: William Morrow and Company, Inc., 1978.

Walsh, Tim. "Wham-O Frisbee" in *The Playmakers: Amazing Origins of Timeless Toys,* pages 137–141. Sarasota, FL: Keys Publishing, 2004.

MAGAZINE & NEWSPAPER ARTICLES

Cooper, Corinne. "The Frisbee Frenzy: Whole New World." *American Collector*, August 1978, pages 12–13 & 31.

Danna, Mark. "After 30 High-Flying Years, The Frisbee Still Soars." *Sports Illustrated,* May 11, 1987.

Flagg, M. J. "Aerodynamics: Secret of the Frisbee Toss." *Science Digest,* June 1978, pages 73, 74–75.

Leonard, George. "Flat Flip Flies Straight." *Esquire Magazine,* February 1988, pages 138–141, 143–146.

Flint, Frank P. "Frisbee: Manners And Morals." *Sports Illustrated,* June 3, 1957, "Letters," page 79.

Flying Disc Magazine. 1980 (3 issues).

Flying Disc World. 1974–1975 (9 issues).

"Flying Frisbees." *Sports Illustrated,* May 13, 1957, "Events & Discoveries," page 22.

"Flying Saucers." *People and Places,* June, 1958, page 22. (DeSoto dealer publication)

"Frisbee." *National Lampoon Magazine,* July 1979, page 32.

Frisbee Disc World. 1976–1981 (31 issues).

"Frisbee for Fanatics." *Esquire,* October 1976, pages 88–89.

"Frisbee: Historians Report." *Princeton Alumni Weekly*, July 1, 1975, "Letters," page 79.

"Frisbee: Ohio Version." *Sports Illustrated,* May 27, 1957, "19th Hole, Readers Take Over" (letters), pages 78–79.

"Frisbee: Phrisbee." *Princeton Alumni Weekly,* July 1, 1975, "Letters," page 79.

"Frisbee Sports & Games." *Boy's Life,* August 1979, page 15.

"From Pie Tin to Frisbee." *National Geographic World,* December 1987..

Gott, Peter H. "The First Frisbee." *Princeton Alumni Weekly,* July 1, 1975, "Letters," page 7.

Higdon, Hal. "Gentlemen, Start Your Frisbees!" *Ford Times* (Dearborn, MI), April 1970, pages 39–43.

IFA News. 1968–1974 (20 issues).

Jares, Joe. "It's Beer, Bratwurst and a Guts Game." *Sports Illustrated,* August 1970, pages 48–49.

Johnson, Stancil. "A Slightly Slanted Pitch on Frisbees." *Smithsonian,* September 1976, pages 179–180.

Makower, Joel. "Pie in the Sky." *New York Post,* October 31, 1985, page 41.

Morrison, Shelley. "From Pie Tin to Rose Bowl." *Young Athlete,* March 1976, pages 70–73.

"Name's Frisbee, The." *Newsweek,* July 8, 1957, "Life And Leisure-Games," page 85.

"One Man's Toy." *Sports Illustrated,* February 26, 1990, page 85.

O'Rourke, P. J. "Play it Where it Lays: Frisbee Golf in Central Park." *New York Times,* June 12, 1977, pages 24–25.

Palmeri, Jim. "Collecting the Pluto Platter." *Flying Disc Magazine,* February 1980, pages 18–22.

Palmeri, Jim. "The Space Saucer." *Flying Disc Magazine,* April/May 1980, pages 46–47.

Peterson, James R. "Zen and the Art of Frisbee." *Oui Magazine,* May 1975, page 88.

Reed, J. D. "They Are My Life and My Wife." *Sports Illustrated,* February 24, 1975, pages 62–72.

Roddick, Dan. "Frisbee Disc Sports—A Game for Everyone." *Journal of the National Intramural Recreational Sports Association,* May 1979, pages 45–47.

Sabin, Lou. "Frisbee's on the Rise." *Boy's Life,* 1975.

Talese, Gay. "Frisbees, Yo Yos, Goo-Goos, Etc." *New York Times Magazine,* August 11, 1957, page 24.

Tidyman, Kathryn. "Frisbee." *Boys Life Magazine,* March 1978, pages 30–33.

Tips, Charles. "Frisbee—Play it Your Way." *Young Athlete,* June 1977, pages 53–55.

"What's Next? Why, Frisbee Golf." *Mechanix Illustrated,* March 1978, page 80.

Wilhelm, Douglas. "Famed Flying Frisbee Feted on its 50th." *The Boston Globe,* June 4, 1989, pages 29–30.

Index

Page numbers for images are in bold italics

Games

Acknowledgements

A special Thank-you to all those who provided motivation, essential research information, editing assistance, and/or graphic materials for this book: **John "Dreamer" "Z" Weyand, Kevin "Skippy Jammer" Givens, Ed Babb, Jack Barry, Frank Logosh, Tom McRann, Dan Mangone, Steve Trauger, Sheryl Newland, Lige Johnson** and...

Pat Kennedy: Her tireless editing assistance got us to the zero-hour printing deadline on time!

Lightnin' Lyle Jensen: Poor Lyle, I drove him crazy with the license I took on proper writing, but he never wavered in his support or attempts to get me to change my ways and write better! Lyle really knows his stuff.

Jake Healy and **Dick Warden:** Two stalwarts from the very foundation of all disc sports! They both agreed to talk with us, supplying exquisite information that allowed us to get the straight scoop on the origin of Guts and the IFT.

Victor Malafronte and **Martin Hain**: The best Frisbee history researchers in all the land! They submitted volumes of obscure information about early Frisbee that revealed valuable insights about the true chain of events that brought us Disc Golf.

Dave Johnson and **Geoff Hungerford**: These guys agreed to assess a very early draft, and came forth with critically important suggestions and editing changes that helped steer the book in the right direction. Critically important, trust me!

George Sappenfield and **Stancil Johnson**: How fortunate for me that I met these two Frisbee icons in 1975. I got to know them very well, and they shared a treasure trove of early Frisbee history and great insider information that only they could know.

Jumpin' Joe Feidt: It was Joe that kick-started this project by adamantly telling me, "Jim, you've got to get off your duff and start writing the book instead of just talking about it." Joe has continued to support our efforts right from the very beginning.

Bob "Flash" Kingsley: Over many years, long discourses with Flash about Frisbee, its history, its impact upon society, and Disc Golf in particular have imparted invaluable concepts that helped shape the development of this book. Flash's ever-present enthusiasm for Frisbee was always with me as I struggled to find the proper wording every step of the way.

Dan "Stork" Roddick: Dan has been my mentor for 41 years; his sage advice and keen insights have kept this book project on track and in reality mode right from the very first sentence. In retrospect, how very propitious it was that Dan won the car!

Phil Kennedy: Anyone who knows me even a little bit knows without a shadow of a doubt that all by myself, I couldn't put a book like this together in a million years! Phil is a master craftsman and graphic artist, adroit editor, Frisbee historian extraordinaire, consummate disc collector and all around great guy to hook up with for any reason. No Phil, no book! It is as simple as that.

And Thank-you to all you avid disc golfers out there: you took this game and exploded it into a great worldwide sport, thus giving us a reason for this book in the first place!

GRAPHIC MATERIALS

Back cover photo of Jim and Phil, by Pat Kennedy, 2015.

All photos of discs, and front cover photo, are ©Phil Kennedy. Digital photos taken with a Canon 5D Mark III. Most images have been digitally enhanced in Adobe Photoshop CS6.

DESIGN & PRODUCTION

This book was designed and produced in Adobe InDesign CS6 on an Apple Power Mac desktop computer running OSX 10.6.8.

Most type fonts are from the Zapf Humanist family.

A FINAL NOTE: While we've endeavored tirelessly to create the perfect masterpiece, inevitably flaws may be lurking. If you find an error or make a historical discovery, please alert us so that we can make the next edition even better!

Order Form

Use for purchases within the U.S. only.

A CHAIN OF EVENTS

The Origin and Evolution of Disc Golf

PLEASE PRINT CLEARLY

Name ____

Address ____

City ____________________________ State ______ Zip______________

Telephone (For order contact only) ______________________________

Email (For order contact only)__________________________________

Please send_______ book(s) @ $19.95 each . . . . $ ___________

Shipping & handling: First book $4.50 . . . . $ ___________

Add'l books @$1.50 each . . . . $ ___________

Sub Total of Above. . . . . $ ___________

Add 4% Sales Tax for orders shipped to NY addresses . . $ ___________

TOTAL . . . . $ ___________

Please fill out a copy of this order form and send with payment to:

WORMHOLE PUBLISHERS
Ordering Dept., 180 Norman Road, Rochester, NY 14623

Money Order / Certified Check allows next day shipping in most cases.
Personal / Business check must clear before shipment (7 to 10 days).

Books will be sent Media Mail.

Order by major credit card or PayPal at: www.FlatFlip.com

For special pricing for bookstores, dealers and distributors,
please email: chain.of.events@outlook.com